BASIC BIBLE DOCTRINES

BASIC BIBLE DOCTRINES

Short Explanations of Some 124 Doctrines and Themes of the Scriptures

by

MILLARD F. DAY

MOODY PRESS
CHICAGO

Printed in the United States of America

INTRODUCTION

The purpose of this work is to combine in one volume the greatest possible number of Bible doctrine explanations, primarily adapted to the needs of untrained Christians, so that they can turn at will to the interpretation of any important doctrine. The explanations are couched in concise, simple language, readily understood by the average layman.

There is no intention of dictating what others shall believe, but of ncorporating what the Bible teaches; for faith must be based on one's own understanding of the Word of God, rather than upon the teachings of men. However, the New Testament in many places particularly emphasizes "sound doctrine"; ignorance of Bible doctrine has been the cause of many well-meaning Christians being drawn into modern heresies and cults.

It is our hope and prayer that this volume will give honor and glory to the blessed Lord Jesus Christ, and that some of God's children may be helped to know and "to speak the things which become sound doctrine."

—MILLARD F. DAY

This work would have been impossible without the almost incalculable assistance derived from the writings of Dr. Harry A. Ironside, Dr. William L. Pettingill, Dr. Arno C. Gaebelein, and Dr. Reuben A. Torrey.

INDEX

9

ABBREVIATIONS

A.D., Anno domini (in the year of our Lord)

A.V., Authorized Version (King James)

B.C., Before Christ

cf., confer (compare)

Gr., Greek

N.T., New Testament

O.T., Old Testament

R.S.V., Revised Standard Version (U.S., 1946)

R.V., Revised Version (Am. Standard Version)

WHAT'S IN THE BIBLE

SALVATION—Salvation is the free gift of God to man, by grace through faith, entirely aside from works: "For by grace you have been saved through faith; and this is not your own doing, it is the gift of God—not because of works, lest any man should boast" (Eph. 2:8, 9, R.S.V.; see also Rom. 3:27, 28; 4:1-8; 6:23). The only condition of salvation is belief on the Lord Jesus Christ. "What must I do to be saved? . . . Believe on the Lord Jesus Christ, and thou shalt be saved . . ." (Acts 16:30, 31). First comes salvation, and then works (Eph. 2:9, 10; Titus 3:5-8).

The salvation offered in this age of grace embodies every aspect of God's grace, such as redemption, propitiation, justification, forgiveness, imputation, sanctification, glorification, and reconciliation.

JUSTIFICATION—Justification is by faith, and not by works (Rom. 3:28-30; 4:5; 5:1; Gal. 2:16; 3:24). Justification starts in grace, and is through the work of redemption and propitiation that is in Christ Jesus (Rom. 3:24, 25; Titus 3:4-7). It is God's just act of counting as righteous everyone who believes on the Lord Jesus Christ (Rom. 4:3-5; 8:33).

REDEMPTION—Redemption is "deliverance by paying a ransom." Sinners are ransomed by the shed blood of Christ, who died in the place of all (Gal. 3:13; II Cor. 5:21; I Tim. 2:6; I Peter 1:18, 19), and all would be saved if they believed on the Lord Jesus Christ (Acts 16:30, 31; see also John 3:18). Our Lord paid on the cross the ransom for our deliverance, while the Holy Spirit makes that deliverance real in the lives of believers (Rom. 8:2, 11).

GRACE—Grace is the limitless love of God expressed in measureless kindness; it is "the kindness and love of God our Saviour toward man, not by works of righteousness which we have done" (Titus 3:4, 5). The dispensation of grace began with Christ's crucifixion and resurrection (Rom. 3:24-26; 4:24, 25), and will continue until He comes again, during which time salvation is solely dependent upon the acceptance of Christ as Saviour (John 1:12, 13; 3:16; 3:36; I John 5:10-12); good works should follow salvation (Eph. 2:10; Titus 2:14; 3:8). Grace manifests itself through the redemption (salvation) in Christ (Rom. 3:24), and also in the daily life of the believer (Rom. 6:15).

GRACE (Imparted)—The believer is to "grow in grace" (II Peter 3:18), for he is not under law, but under grace (Rom. 6:14); and God continuously, through the Holy Spirit, works to bestow on the believer many graces, the ultimate purpose of which is to bring forth Christlikeness in the believer. The most comprehensive record of such graces is found in Galatians 5:22, 23: "But the fruit of the Spirit is love, joy, peace, longsuffering, gentleness, goodness, faith, meekness, temperance [self-control]." These graces are directly associated with (a) Christian service, (b) Christian growth, and (c) giving.

a	b
Romans 12:6	II Corinthians 2:1-12
Romans 15:15, 16	Ephesians 4:29
I Corinthians 1:3-7	Colossians 4:6
I Corinthians 3:10	II Thessalonians 1:12
II Corinthians 12:9, 10	Hebrews 4:16
Galatians 2:9	Hebrews 12:28, 29
Ephesians 3:7, 8	Hebrews 13:9
Philippians 1:7	I Peter 1:2
II Timothy 2:1, 2	I Peter 3:7

c

II Corinthians 4:15
II Corinthians 8:1, 2
II Corinthians 8:6, 7
II Corinthians 9:13

PROPITIATION—The Lord Jesus Christ is our propitiation (I John 2:2; 4:10), through faith in His shed blood (Rom. 3:25). He bore on the cross God's righteous judgment (death) against the sinner, so that by His death God is propitiated and declared righteous when, foreseeing the efficacy of the sacrifice of His Son, He passes over the sins of His people living before the cross (Rom. 3:25), and is declared just during this age when He justifies all who merely believe in Jesus (Rom. 3:26).

IMPUTATION—Imputation is the divine authorization of God, to account (impute) as righteousness man's belief in Christ (James 2:23); and by this act the saved are said to have been "made" the righteousness of God (I Cor. 1:30; II Cor. 5:21). In Paul's letter to Philemon (vv. 17, 18), there is an excellent illustration of merit imputed and demerit imputed. Paul writes: "If thou count me therefore a partner, receive him [Onesimus] as myself [merit]; and if he hath wronged thee, or oweth thee ought, put that on mine account [demerit]."

FORGIVENESS AND CONFESSION—Forgiveness (remission) is by the shed blood of Christ (Matt. 26:28), and is to disunite sin from the sinner. There is much difference between human and divine forgiveness; human forgiveness is to remit the penalty. Divine forgiveness is to all who be-

15

lieve in Christ (Acts 10:43); the penalty was paid in our stead by Him on the cross; for without the shedding of blood there is no divine forgiveness (remission) (Heb. 9:22). When a believer sins, his fellowship with the Father and the Son is disrupted; but God forgives us these sins upon confession, and cleanses us from all unrighteousness (I John 1:6-9); but only through Jesus Christ the righteous as our propitiation (I John 2:1, 2). In human forgiveness, believers are called upon to forgive one another, even as God for Christ's sake has forgiven them (Eph. 4:32).

SANCTIFICATION—Sanctified, or holy, means "set apart unto God." Both words are employed in each Testament of places, days, and inanimate things, as well as of persons. When used of persons there are three primary meanings: (1) *positionally*, believers are eternally "sanctified through the offering of the body of Jesus Christ once for all" (Heb. 10:10), being set apart from all that is unholy, and becoming saints, at the instant of their belief (Phil. 1:1; Heb. 3:1). Though positionally sanctified, holy, and hence saints of God, this positional sanctification does not mean that believers are sanctified or holy in their daily lives. This type of sanctification is entirely separate—it may be called (2) *experimental sanctification*, in which are embodied the daily life phases of sanctification and holiness, depending upon (a) separation from sin, brought about by the power of the indwelling Holy Spirit (Rom. 8:4; Gal. 5:16); (b) yieldedness to God (Rom. 12:1); and (c) Christian growth achieved (II Peter 3:18). (3) In consummation, the final, finished sanctification awaits believers at the coming of the Lord Jesus Christ, when "we shall be like him; for we shall see him as he is" (I John 3:2).

FAITH—Faith is that trust which does not ask to know all about God, but believes all that God has said; it is that belief which is the sole condition of salvation (Acts 16:30, 31), the belief which receives Christ as Saviour and Lord (John 1:12), and takes the form of confessing with the mouth while believing in the heart (Rom. 10:9, 10), influencing the saved to humble and loving obedience and meritorious works (James 2:14-26). The faith of salvation is the complete trust in the Lord Jesus Christ as having been "delivered for our transgressions and raised again for our justification" (Rom. 4:20-25), entirely aside from works. By faith God gives the soul assurance and conviction of the reality of things never yet seen by the natural eye (Heb. 11:1-3).

The triumphs of faith in the daily life are marvelously illustrated for the believer in Hebrews 11:1-39. For prayer, the believer is to "come boldly to the throne of grace" (Heb. 4:16), where faith is "the confidence in him, that if we ask anything according to his will, he heareth us, . . . and we know that we have the petitions that we desired of him" (I John 5:14, 15). Faith comes by hearing, and hearing by the Word of God (Rom. 10:17).

ASSURANCE—Assurance is by faith (Heb. 10:22), and is the believer's confidence that all who believe on the name of the Son of God have eternal life (I John 5:13), a salvation in which he will be safely held forever. Assurance rests completely upon the abiding evidence of the infallible Word of God.

REPENTANCE—The Greek word translated "repentance" in the English New Testament means a "change of mind," and actually implies a complete reversal of the inward attitude toward self, toward sin, toward God, and toward Christ. This change of attitude was commanded by God (Matt. 3:2; 4:17; Luke 13:3). Reformation, turning over a new leaf, is not repentance; neither is penitence (sorrow be-

17

cause of sin), though godly sorrow, it is said, works repent-ance (II Cor. 7:8-11); nor is penance (the attempt to atone for sin committed). The possession of saving faith will not put an end to repentance, but saving faith does embrace repentance. True repentance is portrayed by the son in Matthew 21:28, 29.

RECONCILIATION—Reconciliation occurs when man's enmity toward God is removed and a complete reversal of attitude is worked in man, from hatred to love and faith (Rom. 5:10; Eph. 2:16). God is never reconciled to man—man is reconciled to God (II Cor. 5:18-21).

THE NEW BIRTH (Born Again)—"Ye must be born again!" (John 3:7). Who? *Everyone*, in order to enter into the kingdom of God; in order to be saved. The old natural birth does not count; it must be a *new spiritual birth*. The Lord Jesus Christ says, "Except a man be born of water and of the Spirit, he cannot enter into the kingdom of God" (John 3:5). What did He mean? We search the Bible and find that water is the symbol for the Word of God ("born of water" here has nothing to do with water baptism, as baptism speaks of death, not birth), *so man must be born again of the Holy Spirit, using the Word of God*. The Lord makes it very clear that there is a great distinction between the flesh and the Spirit when He says, "That which is born of the flesh is flesh; and that which is born of the Spirit is spirit" (John 3:6); flesh remains flesh to the very end.

The Lord explains that there are mysteries in nature which we cannot understand: "The wind blows where it wills, and you hear the sound of it, but you do not know whence it comes or whither it goes; so it is with every one who is born of the Spirit" (John 3:8, R.S.V.). You cannot see the wind, but you recognize its power; you cannot see the Holy Spirit, but you recognize His power. He is invisible, but He makes His presence felt in a mighty way as He convicts and regenerates sinful men. He changes men completely; you recognize the power, although you do not see it actually working; you see a vain, worldly woman suddenly become a quiet woman of prayer; you see a wicked, godless man changed into a saint; *they become new creatures in Christ Jesus,* with new desires, new hopes, new ambitions, and new hatreds too; for they hate the old things in which they used to live. That is the work of the Holy Spirit. You do not see the Spirit, but you see the power manifest in the life. In view of these truths we conclude that: (a) God requires the new birth in man because the natural man (I Cor. 2:14) cannot understand spiritual things; they are foolishness to him, no matter how educated, cultured or moral he may be; he entirely lacks the ability to "enter into the kingdom of God" (John 3:5), being absolutely unable to obey or please God (Rom. 8:7, 8). (b) Turning over a new leaf is not the new birth, the new birth being a creation of the Holy Spirit (John 1:12, 13; 3:5; II Cor. 5:17; Eph. 2:10; 4:24); not by producing "happy feelings" or ecstatic "experiences," but solely by believing the Word of God; the Holy Spirit opens the Word to man's spirit, as he hears and reads; he is made to understand his present relationship to God and his high destiny, learning that he who was once alien and outcast is now, through infinite grace, a child of God and joint heir with Christ (Rom. 8:16, 17). (c) The requirement for the new birth is belief on Christ crucified and risen (John 1:12, 13; 3:14, 15; Gal. 3:24), and it occurs at the instant of belief. (d) Through the new birth the believer lives in Christ, and Christ in the believer (Gal. 2:20; Eph. 2:10; 4:24; I Peter 1:23-25; I John 5:10-12).

In summation, it is the Word of God received by faith and engrafted in the heart by the Holy Spirit that produces the new birth.

GIVING—Giving is one of the graces, a spontaneous desire from a loving heart, created by the Holy Spirit (II Cor. 8:7). (a) Under the law, tithing was a divine requisite, but under grace, Christian giving is voluntary. The doctrine of Christian giving is clearly set forth in chapters 8 and 9 of II Corinthians. (b) Believers themselves must be given to the Lord (8:5). (c) Believers' giving proves the sincerity of their love (8:8). (d) Whatever has been promised is to be given (8:10, 11). (e) Rich and poor alike have the privilege of giving in proportion to ability to do so (8:12-15). (f) To give sparingly is to reap sparingly, and giving is not to be grudgingly, for God loves a cheerful giver (9:6, 7). (g) God takes account of believers' giving, and is able and willing to see that all grace shall abound toward those who give with willing hearts (8:8-11). (h) Finally, it should be remembered that no one can give beyond His giving (8:9; 9:15).

THE CHURCH—The word *church* as used in the New Testament means a called-out or assembled body of people. It has two applications:

(a) The visible or local church (I Cor. 1:2; Gal. 1:2; I Tim. 3:15); a gathering of professed believers, but not necessarily Christians, existing under various names, maintaining many differences in doctrine, and known to the world as "the church."

(b) The true Church; that company of people being gathered by the Holy Spirit into one Body, of which Christ is the Head (I Cor. 12:12, 13; Eph. 1:22, 23), which company includes only those born-again people from Pentecost to the first resurrection (I Cor. 15:52), regardless of nationality, whether Jew or Gentile (Col. 3:11), and seen in Heaven as the Bride of the Lamb, forever reigning with the King and forever sharing in His glory (Rev. 19:7, 8; 21:9).

RESURRECTION—The Lord Jesus Christ predicted His own bodily resurrection (John 2:18-22); He is the first to rise from the dead, the "firstfruits" (I Cor. 15:20). Dead persons have been restored to life (II Kings 4:32-35; 13:21; Matt. 9:25; Luke 7:12-15; John 11:43, 44; Acts 9:36-41), but only to their former existences, and so were again subject to death. The Lord Jesus Christ's resurrection was in His eternal, glorified body, which type of body is promised to all believers at His coming again (Phil. 3:20, 21).

Two resurrections are yet to come, of "all that are in the graves" (John 5:28); the first, designated the resurrection "of life," the second, that "of condemnation" (John 5:29). Between them will be the millennial period of one thousand years (Rev. 20:5). The first resurrection is in three parts: the resurrection of Christ as the firstfruits (I Cor. 15:20-23), the resurrection of the saved at the Rapture (I Thess. 4:13-18), and the resurrection of the martyrs of the Great Tribulation (Rev. 20:4-6), occurring at His second coming to the earth (I Cor. 15:23).

The resurrection body of the saved in a sense will be the same body rising in another form (I Cor. 15:37, 38). It will be incorruptible, spiritual, glorious, powerful (I Cor. 15:42, 44, 49), instead of the old body of humiliation that went into the grave. The bodies of the living saints will be instantly changed (I Cor. 15:50-53; Phil. 3:20, 21); this change and resurrection are known as the "redemption of the body" (Rom. 8:23).

Following the Millennium will be the resurrection of the lost, the "rest of the dead" (Rev. 20:5), who will be judged at the Great White Throne and condemned forever (Rev. 20:11-15). This contradicts any false impression of a "general resurrection." Nothing is known of the resurrection body of the unsaved

21

THE RESURRECTION BODY—It will not be the same body that is laid in the grave (I Cor. 15:35-38), neither will it be flesh and blood (I Cor. 15:50, 51), nor will it be pure spirit; but it will have flesh and bones (Luke 24:39; cf. Phil. 3:21). It will be incorruptible and imperishable (I Cor. 15:42). It will be a glorious body and powerful (I Cor. 15:43); the times of weariness and weakness will be forever at an end; this glorious and powerful body will be able to accomplish all that the Spirit purposes. As the first body was earthy, so will this body be heavenly (I Cor. 15:47-49), bright like the sun (Matt. 13:43; 17:2; Dan. 12:3); it has been conjectured that the bodies of Adam and Eve were so before they sinned, and that this glory served as a covering which departed when they fell, and so "they knew that they were naked" (Gen. 3:7). They will be "like the angels"; they do not marry, neither can they die any more (Matt. 22:30; Luke 20:35, 36). Resurrection bodies will differ from one another in degrees of glory (I Cor. 15:41, 42). The resurrection body will be the consummation of our adoption; in the resurrection body it will be outwardly manifest that we are sons of God. Before His incarnation, Christ was "in the form of God" (Phil. 2:6), that is, in the visible appearance of God; and so shall we be in the resurrection (cf. Col. 3:4, R.V.; I John 3:2, R.V.).

DEATH—Man became subject to physical and spiritual death as a result of sin (Gen. 2:17; 3:19).

Adam's initial sin falls upon every member of the human race, with the same sentence of death resting upon all (Rom. 5:12-14). In physical death the body dies, but life itself continues on (Luke 16:19-31; Rev. 6:9-11); the resurrection of the body is the ultimate termination of death (I Cor. 15:52; I Thess. 4:16). Not all of the saved suffer physical death (Gen. 5:24; I Cor. 15:51, 52; I Thess. 4:15-17). In Scripture physical death is known as "sleep," the rising of the body in resurrection being similar to awaking and capable of occurring at any moment (Phil. 3:20, 21; I Thess. 4:14-18). Physical death is the separation of soul and spirit from the body, which is the house of soul and spirit, called in Scripture the "tent" or "tabernacle," in which one lives (II Cor. 5:1-8; II Peter 1:13, 14). At death the saved immediately depart to be with the Lord, which is "far better" (Phil. 1:23), being "clothed upon" with a "house which is from heaven," in which to await the resurrection of the earthly body (II Cor. 5:1, 8).

Spiritual death is eternal separation of soul and spirit from God (Eph. 2:1; 2:5). It is the natural man's condition in sin, alienated from God through his ignorance and blindness of heart (Eph. 4:18, 19). Spiritual death continues after physical death into a conscious existence of suffering for eternity, separated from God, in what Scripture calls the "lake of fire" and the "second death" (Rev. 2:11; 20:6, 14; 21:8). The "second death" is not annihilation, for the Beast and False Prophet are both alive and conscious in this "lake of fire," though cast into it one thousand years before (Rev. 19:20; 20:10).

SIN—Sin has many manifestations, and may be said to be any and all falling short of the glory of God, whether in thought, word or deed. Among the translations in the New Testament from the Greek word meaning sin are the following: *transgression*, a violation of the law (Luke 15:29; Gal. 3:19); *iniquity*, an evil or wicked act (Acts 8:22, 23); *disobedience*, neglect or refusal to obey (Heb. 2:2); *trespass*, an encroachment upon God's authority (Eph. 2:1); *lawlessness*, the complete denial of any rule in life (I Tim. 1:9); *unbelief*, a denial and insult to the truth of God's Word (Heb. 3:12; John 16:9).

23

Sin in the world began with the fall of Adam, instigated by Satan (Rom. 5:12; Gen. 3:1-5). Death, physical and spiritual, entered the world through sin and passed upon all men (Rom. 5:12), in that all men are sinners (Rom. 3:23). The only cure is belief on the Lord Jesus Christ (Acts 16: 30, 31).

Three classifications of sin may be enumerated: the *sin nature*, disobedience and enmity to God (Rom. 5:19); the *sin state*, complete lack of merit or righteousness (Rom. 11:32; Gal. 3:22); the *sin act*, everything in the daily life coming short of the character of God (Rom. 3:23).

SIN UNTO DEATH—The "sin unto death" and the "sin not unto death" of I John 5:16, 17 are to be understood in the light of the doctrine taught in I Corinthians 11:31, 32. Physical death is sometimes a judicial penalty from God visited upon His saved people for unconfessed, unjudged sin. When a Christian falls into sin, his salvation is not jeopardized, but his fellowship with God is interrupted. The way back into fellowship is through confession (I John 1:9). If God's child, in such circumstances, refuses to confess, the Father is forced to chasten him. The Corinthian Christians were in just such a case. They had been disorderly in the observance of the Lord's Supper, eating the bread and drinking the cup unworthily, that is, in an unworthy manner, and were thus guilty of the body and the blood of the Lord (I Cor. 11:27). They refused to examine themselves in order that they might so eat of the bread and drink of the cup as to please God (v. 28). They continued to eat and drink unworthily, eating and drinking judgment unto themselves, not discerning the Lord's body (v. 29).

For this cause many were weak and sickly among them, and many had fallen asleep; that is to say, they had died under the chastening hand of God. They were still saved, but physical death had been visited upon them in chastening (v. 30). Had they judged themselves, they would not have been judged by Him (v. 31), but since they had compelled Him to judge them, they had been chastened of the Lord that they should not be condemned with the world (v. 32).

Condemnation is impossible for those who are in Jesus Christ (Rom. 8:1, R.V.); they have already been condemned in the person of their Substitute and put to death on the cross of Calvary; and now, since they have become God's children by the new birth, they can never again be brought under condemnation. But they can be chastened, even to physical illness or physical death. Moses sinned unto death (Deut. 32:48-52); Achan committed a sin unto death (Josh. 7:16-26); and Ananias and Sapphira committed a sin unto death (Acts 5:1-11).

GOSPEL—The word *gospel* means "good news," and four types of the gospel are found in the New Testament.

(1) The gospel of the kingdom; preached first by John the Baptist (Matt. 3:1, 2), followed by the preaching of the Lord Jesus Christ (Matt. 4:23), and His disciples (Matt. 10:7), terminating when the King was crucified. It constitutes the setting up on earth and fulfilling the Davidic Covenant (II Sam. 7:16), a political and spiritual world kingdom, its capital Jerusalem; with the heir to the throne of David, the Lord Jesus Christ, as King; it will last through the millennial period of one thousand years and subject the world to a truly just and righteous rule, such as it had never known before. There is to be yet another preaching of this gospel of the kingdom (Matt. 24:14), by the Jewish remnant in the days of the Great Tribulation, before the return of the Lord Jesus Christ in power and glory.

(2) The gospel of the grace of God; this is the gospel of personal salvation by grace through faith for all who believe

that Jesus Christ died on the cross for our sins, and was raised again for our justification. This form of the gospel goes under many names in the New Testament, such as: the "gospel of God" (Rom. 1:1; I Thess. 2:2); the "gospel of Christ" (Mark 1:1; Rom. 1:16); the "gospel of the grace of God" (Acts 20:24); the "gospel of peace" (Eph. 6:15); the "gospel of your salvation" (Eph. 1:13); the "glorious gospel" (II Cor. 4:4). Strictly speaking, the preaching of this gospel started from Christ's death and resurrection, and will continue until the Church is caught up to meet Him in the air.

(3) The everlasting gospel (Rev. 14:6); this gospel will be preached on earth just before Christ's return in glory to set up His earthly throne and judge the nations (Matt. 25: 31, 32). Though it cannot be a gospel of salvation, nor exactly the gospel of the kingdom, it nevertheless means salvation to countless thousands, both Jews and Gentiles, in the Great Tribulation (Rev. 7:9-14).

(4) Paul's "my gospel" (Rom. 2:16); this is that same gospel of personal salvation by grace through faith, but is also inclusive of all divine revelations to Paul regarding the Church, found interspersed in all of Paul's letters.

(5) "Another gospel which is not another" (Gal. 1:6, 7; II Cor. 11:4); Paul warns against perverting the gospel of Christ, and pronounces (Gal. 1:8, 9) a curse upon man or angel who preaches any other gospel. There have been many perversions—law in Galatia, angel-worship in Colosse (Col. 2:18), and others. Paul's language is solemn, and has echoed down through the centuries: "let him be accursed" who preaches any other gospel.

MAN—HIS CREATION—Man was the consummation of God's creation (I Cor. 2:11, 12); he was created, generally speaking, in God's image and likeness (Gen. 1:26, 27), and specifically from the dust of the ground. God breathed into his nostrils the breath of life and man became a living soul (Gen. 2:7). This was clearly an act of divine creation, not evolution, and is so stated by God and verified by the Lord Jesus (Matt. 19:4; Mark 10:6).

Man is a tripartite being, spirit, soul and body (I Thess. 5:23), which principally constitutes his image of and likeness to God. Spirit is the part of man able to contemplate God, the part that knows (I Cor. 2:11) and is capable of distinguishing. Soul is the part of man embodying the sensibilities (Ps. 42:1-6), emotions, affections, desires, etc., and will. The "heart," as used in Scripture, is practically the same as soul. Soul, too, is frequently used as the individual person (Gen. 2:7; 12:5). The physical body, subject to death, is the earthly abode of soul and spirit, and embodies the physical senses, the consciousness of which is conveyed to soul and spirit. The body of the saved, with soul and spirit, will be redeemed and forever glorified at the resurrection (I Cor. 15:47-50). The unsaved will be raised one thousand years later to a judgment of eternal condemnation (Rev. 20:11-15).

CREATION AND FORMING OF MAN—"So God created man in his own image" (Gen. 1:27). *Creation* implies bringing into existence that which did not exist before, material things out of nothing. Three times in Genesis 1 it is said that God *created*; in verse 1 there is the creation of the universe; in verse 21 the creation of animal life; in verse 27 the creation of man, involving a human spirit. The living did not evolve from the "non-living," and the spirit did not evolve from animal life; there is a distinct act of *creation* in each case.

"And the Lord formed man out of the dust of the ground" (Gen. 2:7). To *form* is to make from that which already exists; so God *created* man by bringing the human spirit into existence; but He *formed* the body of man from that which already existed, the dust of the earth.

THE FALL OF MAN—The fall of man is narrated in Genesis 3 as a fact, and the whole narrative is psychologically faithful to human experience. The scriptural view of sin and redemption takes the Fall for granted. God created man, male and female, "endued them with living, reasonable and immortal souls; made them after His own image, in knowledge, righteousness and holiness, having the law of God written in their hearts, and power to fulfill it, . . . yet subject to fall" (Larger Catechism 17). But upon being left to the freedom of their will, they yielded to temptation and thus transgressed the commandment of God (Gen. 2:16, 17; 3:1-8). Through their disobedience they fell from the state of innocency and sinlessness. The result of the Fall is universal sin, which has been conveyed to posterity by natural generation so that all human beings are conceived and born in sin (Ps. 51:5; John 3:6; Rom. 5:12). Death—spiritual, temporal, and eternal—is the consequence of sin. Many exegetes see in Genesis 3:15 the first announcement of the gospel of redemption. The narrative includes also much symbolism of human suffering connected with the Fall (Gen. 3:16-19).

Paul assumes that there is no need of proof that man's sinfulness is the result of Adam's fall. Just as Adam is related to the race as the author of sin and death, so Christ is the author of righteousness and life. At one end are Adam and sinful humanity; at the other, Christ and redeemed humanity (Rom. 5:12-21; I Cor. 15:21, 22, 45-49).

MAN—THE NEW AND OLD—In Romans 6:6, the "old man" is the unsaved man with all his evil desires and habits, the natural man himself. That man was crucified with Christ, and is seen by God on that cross with His blessed Son. God counts the old man dead, and the believer is urged to make this so in actuality by "putting off" the old and "putting on" the new man (Col. 3:8-14).

But the "new man" (Eph. 4:24) is the born-again man, and he who was crucified with Christ now lives with Christ (Gal. 2:20), and Christ in him. This "new man" is not a reformation, but is a new creation (II Cor. 5:17; Gal. 6:15), a partaker of the divine nature (II Peter 1:4).

MAN'S NATURE—Man in the beginning was created a tripartite being. Hebrews 4:12 shows that soul and spirit of man are capable of being divided, thus proving they are not the same. Neither is the natural physical body (*soma psuchikon* in the Greek) the same as the resurrection body, which is a spiritual body (Greek, *soma pneumatikon*) (I Cor. 15:44), though it consists of flesh and bones (Luke 14:39). There is a vast difference between soul and spirit in Scripture, the spirit being the part of man capable of knowing and distinguishing (I Cor. 2:11), in brief, the mind; whereas the soul constitutes the part of man which embraces the sensibilities, such as emotions, affections, desires, and the will, being similar to the "heart," as used of Scripture (Matt. 26:38; 11:29; John 12:27). The Hebrew word *nephesh* in the Old Testament, translated *soul,* is alike in meaning to the Greek word *psuche* of the New Testament, and the uses of the words are the same. The Hebrew word in the Old Testament for spirit is *ruach,* the Greek word in the New Testament being *pneuma;* and each is rendered by the translators *wind, air, breath,* but for the most part *spirit,* both of God and of men. Man, being spirit, has awareness of God, and may, if saved, commune with God through prayer (Ps. 65:2; Acts 10:31; James 5:15). Being soul, man has awareness of self (Ps. 42:5, 6), and being body man has through the senses power of physical perception, which is transmitted to soul and spirit.

MAN'S ORIGINAL CONDITION—God created man in His own image, after His own likeness (Gen. 1:26, 27; 9:6); by reference to Ephesians 4:23, 24; Colossians 3:10; Romans 8:29; II Corinthians 3:18; Colossians 1:15 it is evident that the "image" and "likeness" plainly have reference to the intellectual and moral nature of man; but in Psalm 17:15 (R.V.) the Hebrew word used here clearly means a visible form (cf. Num. 12:8, R.V.), wherefore it would seem that the image and likeness would have also some reference to the *visible* likeness. It is true that God is essentially spirit (John 4:24) and invisible (Col. 1:15); but God has a form in which He manifests Himself to the eye (Isa. 6:1; Acts 7:56; Phil. 2:6). Man seems to have been created not only in the intellectual and moral likeness of God, but in the visible likeness as well (cf. Gen. 5:1, 3). It is impossible to say just how much of this visible likeness was lost by the Fall; but in the regeneration man is not only recreated intellectually and morally in the likeness of God (Eph. 4:23, 24; Col. 3:10), but when the regeneration is complete (at the resurrection), in the outward, visible likeness as well (cf. Phil. 3:21). A comparison of John 17:5 with Philippians 2:6 shows that "the form" of Christ was the form of God.

Man was not created an ignoramus, nor a savage, but a being with lofty intellectual powers, for he gave names to all the living creatures and had dominion over them (Gen. 2:19; 1:28). The doctrine of evolution breaks down completely when applied to man. It contradicts not only Scripture but the known facts of history. The belief that man came from a low order of intellectual beings closely resembling the ape is a figment of unbridled imagination falsely dubbed "science." There is absolutely not one fact to sustain it; the very first view we get of man is of a being of splendid intellect.

FLESH—"Flesh," used in its ethical sense, embraces spirit, soul and body, the entire composition of the unregenerate, natural man, antagonistic to God and Christ (Rom. 7:18). The mark of a true Christian, one not "in the flesh," is the indwelling by the Spirit of God, and if so indwelt he is "in the Spirit" (Rom. 8:9); if, however, the flesh is still in him, he continues to "walk in the flesh," and is a "carnal" Christian. To walk in the Spirit is to overcome the flesh and so please God (Rom. 8:8), and is the constant experience of the "spiritual" Christian (Rom. 8:2-4; Gal. 5:16-18).

THREE TYPES OF HUMANITY—Scripture places man in three classifications, natural, carnal and spiritual.

(1) The natural man is one who is simply born according to nature, never having been regenerated through the new birth. He may be cultured, refined, intellectual, kind and gentle, but still be absolutely destitute of all knowledge of the spiritual truth of Scripture (I Cor. 2:14).

(2) The carnal (lit., fleshly) man, who may be said to be a "fleshly" believer, is born-again, but a follower "after the flesh," a babe in Christ, still feeding on "milk" and not yet able to eat "meat" (I Cor. 3:1-4), being still unable to comprehend the deeper things of Scripture.

(3) The spiritual man is a believer, understanding the difference between the things of God and the things of man (I Cor. 2:11, 12), filled with the Holy Spirit and in full fellowship with God in his daily life (Eph. 5:18-20).

SABBATH—The Sabbath (rest) was the divinely instituted day of rest at the completion of creation (Gen. 2:2, 3). From the Creation to the Exodus, more than twenty-five hundred years, no further mention of it is made, when God revealed the Sabbath for man (Exod. 16:23) and proclaimed it a sign and a covenant forever between Himself and Israel

(Exod. 31:13-17). The day was established as one of complete rest and refreshment for Israel, even to the ordering by God of the death sentence to enforce it (Exod. 35:2, 3). The Lord Jesus Christ said, "The Sabbath was made for man, and not man for the sabbath" (Mark 2:27), thus showing conclusively that God never intended it as a day for religious services or worship, but only as a day of rest for man and beast. In the days when the Lord Jesus walked the earth, the Pharisees had applied the law to so many nonessential and trivial acts (Matt. 12:2) that He Himself was classed as a breaker of the Sabbath.

Rightfully, there should be no observance of the seventh day Sabbath during this age, but it is to be observed again during the Millennium (Isa. 66:23). In this age the first day of the week is observed, it being the observation of our Lord's resurrection. The Sabbath is the memorial of God's completed creation; and in the New Testament, aside from the four Gospels, the few times the Sabbath is referred to in Acts is relative to the Jews, while the other references (Col. 2:16 and Heb. 4:4) explain that the seventh day Sabbath is not a day for Christian observance.

THE LORD'S DAY—The day especially associated with the Lord Jesus Christ. The expression occurs but once in the New Testament, where John says, "I was in the Spirit on the Lord's day" (Rev. 1:10). Various interpretations have been offered: (1) John, it is said, is speaking of the Sabbath or seventh day of the week, which God Himself has called "my holy day" (Isa. 58:13); but if he intended the seventh day, it is strange that he did not use the customary designation. (2) It is contended that the expression "Lord's day" is the same as the "day of the Lord" in II Peter 3:10, where it undoubtedly means the day of the second advent; and John would state that he was rapt, in vision, to the day of judgment. But John is apparently dating his vision. (3) John (Rev. 1:9) mentions the place where he was when he received the revelation, the Isle of Patmos, and declares the cause of his being on that island. In this sentence he states the day when he had the vision. It is also to be noticed that he does not speak of the day of the Lord, which is the constant designation of the day of the second advent (II Peter 3:10), but uses the adjective *kyriake*, a distinction which was observed ever afterward between the day of the second advent and the first day of the week when Christ rose from the dead. (4) A special honor, however, was reserved by the apostles for Sunday or resurrection day. On the resurrection day itself our Lord appeared to His disciples (Luke 24:13-49; John 20:1-26). After eight days, which in ordinary usage meant a week, Jesus a second time honored the first day of the week.

Since Pentecost occurred fifty days after the second day of unleavened bread (Lev. 23:11, 15), it probably fell on the first day of the week in the year of Christ's crucifixion; and so the effusion of the Holy Spirit took place on the first day of the week (Acts 2:1). The Christians at Troas in Paul's time seem to have regarded that day as the stated one on which they were to assemble to break bread (20:7). On the same day of the week the Christians were to lay by them in store the money which they designed to give in charity (I Cor. 16:2). These passages, aided by more general principles, have led the great majority of Christians to consider the Lord's day a day set apart by the example of our Lord and His apostles for sacred purposes. The weekly observance points back of Corinth to Jewish-Christian soil, but we cannot say when the custom began. The use of Sunday as the one distinctive day for worship was a matter of gradual development. At first the Jewish Christians observed both the Sabbath and the Lord's day, but the Gentile Christians were not bound to observe the Jewish Sabbath. Even though the Sabbath was not observed by Gentile Christians, they were not ignorant of its deeper meaning, and gradually the essential principles of the Sabbath passed into the Christian sacred day of rest and worship.

BAPTISM—Baptism is for believers; it is not for the unsaved.

Water baptism does not in any way add to our salvation, nor does it in any way enter into it. We are saved by faith and by grace through faith, and on the ground of the shed blood of Christ; and this, not only from our *original sin,* but from *all sin,* and from all our *sins.* The teaching that water baptism in any way atones for our sins is unscriptural. The expression "he that believeth and is baptized shall be saved" (Mark 16·16) doubtless has to do with the kingdom age rather than with the Church age. Note the context: "But he that believeth not shall be damned. And these signs shall follow them that believe; in my name shall they cast out demons; they shall speak with new tongues; they shall take up serpents; and if they drink any deadly thing it shall not hurt them, they shall lay hands on the sick and they shall recover." These signs surely do not always follow faith in the Lord Jesus Christ in the present age. Some Bible teachers believe they are kingdom age signs.

The Lord Jesus Christ fulfilled all righteousness for us when He died, was buried, and rose from the dead. Baptism symbolizes all that, and when a believer submits himself for water baptism, and is buried under the water as a dead man, and then raised up again as in resurrection, he is proclaiming his faith in Christ's death, burial, and resurrection, as the means by which he is saved. By immersion only can this symbolization be properly portrayed, in this writer's opinion.

That baptism meant death, to be followed by resurrection,

34

can be seen from our Lord's saying to James and John (Mark 10:38, R. V.): "You know not what you ask. Are you able to drink the cup that I drink? or to be baptized with the baptism that I am baptized with?" He also says (Luke 12:50, R. V.): "I have a baptism to be baptized with; and how am I straitened [pressed with anguish, Williams] till it be accomplished!" In Matthew (chapter 3) the Lord Jesus is baptized by John, in the River Jordan; and when John would have prevented it, He said (v.15): "Suffer me now· for thus it becometh us to fulfill all righteousness."

This speaks of a symbol, a type, as the Lord Jesus actually fulfilled all righteousness for us when He died on the cross, was buried, and rose in resurrection; so water baptism symbolizes all this, and it may be said that the sinner fulfills all righteousness when he dies and is buried (is buried beneath the water), and is raised in resurrection (is raised up from beneath the water); this is told us by the apostle Paul in Romans 6:4, 5, where he says: "We were buried therefore with him through baptism into death. that like as Christ was raised from the dead through the glory of the Father, so we also might walk in newness of life. For if we have become united with him in the likeness of his death, we shall be also in the likeness of his resurrection" (R. V.); and in Colossians 2:12: "Buried with him in baptism . . . you were also raised with him through faith in the working of God, who raised him from the dead" (R. V.). *Baptism by immersion* would more accurately symbolize (typify) His death, burial and resurrection, it seems to me.

As further proof· in Acts 8:38, 39 Philip and the eunuch "went down into the water" for baptism; John baptized in the River Jordan, where it speaks of the Lord Jesus "coming up out of the water" (Mark 1·10); and John was baptizing at Aenon near Salim, because there was "much" water there

(John 3:23). Why was "much" water to be desired, and why not baptize at one of the numerous and nearby wells, if sprinkling were to be used? The answer, it seems, is apparent.

PRIESTHOOD—In the absence of an organized priesthood, and until the law came, family heads or patriarchs were the family priests, such as Noah, Abraham, Jacob (Gen. 8:20; 26:25; 31:54). At Sinai it was proclaimed by God that Israel should be unto Him a "kingdom of priests" (Exod. 19:6); but God was forced, because of Israel's disobedience, to isolate the priesthood in Aaron and his family (Exod. 28:1). But now, all believers are a holy, a royal priesthood (I Peter 2:5, 9), to offer up sacrifice of praise, the fruit of their lips, giving thanks to His name (Heb. 13:15), also the sacrifice of their living bodies (Rom. 10:1; Phil. 2:17; II Tim. 4:6; I John 3:16), and the sacrifice of their material possessions (Heb. 13:16; Rom. 12:13; Gal. 6:6; III John 5-8); privileges for all believers. Israel had failed in all this. The believer is therefore, a priest by divine right, even as were Aaron's descendants (Heb. 5:1). During the old dispensation, priests had no access into the holiest; only the high priest went in, once a year (Heb. 9:7); but by the death of the Lord Jesus on the cross, the veil between man and God was rent (Heb. 10:20), and now the priesthood of believers are exhorted to enter in spirit where He, the great High Priest, has gone, in full assurance of faith (Heb. 10:19-22).

HELL AND HADES—(1) The word translated "Hell" in the English New Testament is from the Greek *geenna* (Gehenna), being that part of the valley of Hinnom where children were burned as offerings to the god Molech (II Chron. 33:6; Jer. 7:31). The word *Hell* and the place are synonymous with "lake of fire" (Rev. 19:20; 20:10), the final abode of the lost.

(2) The Greek *Hades* of the New Testament, so ofte. misquoted *hell,* is the same as the Hebrew *Sheol* of the Old Testament, being to the ancients the place of the dead, or departed spirits, until the resurrection.

(a) Before Christ's ascension, Hades was in two sections, one the place of the spirits of the saved, the other that of the spirits of the lost, the former called "paradise" and "Abraham's bosom." This is clearly illustrated in the account of Lazarus and the rich man of Luke 16:19-31. At death Lazarus was carried by angels to Abraham's bosom (v. 22); how the rich man arrived in Hades is not told, though he was said to be in torment (v. 23). He was in anguish, while Lazarus was comforted (v. 25). The section of the saved was separated from that of the lost by a great gulf, or chasm (v. 26). The rich man was conscious, in full possession of his mental powers and also of his senses, for he suffered. He is the picture of all the lost in Hades.

(b) Since Christ's ascension, there has been a great change in Hades. Paradise is now the third heaven (II Cor. 12:1-4), and is with God. The point of transition when Paradise and all its inhabitants were removed from Hades to Heaven is quite evidently (Eph. 4:7-10) when Christ ascended up on high, leading a multitude of captives; so that during the age of grace all the saved who die are "at home with the Lord" (II Cor. 5:8). The lost, however, still remain in Hades, Scripture recording no change in their situation; but Scripture does record that Hades will give up its dead for the judgment of the Great White Throne, after which they will with Hades be thrown into the lake of fire, Hell.

SATAN—This terrific personage was probably created the greatest being of all God's creatures. Of his personality and existence we have the evidence of highest authority, the Lord Jesus Christ, that he is not merely an evil influence or principle but a real person, as the Scriptures attest. He is a person of great dignity (Jude 8, 9), originally created perfect, falling from his high estate through pride (Isa. 14: 12-14). He appeared to Adam and Eve through the medium of the serpent, and by tempting Eve brought about the fall of Adam and the human race, introducing sin into the world. Unlike the fallen angels of Jude 6, he is free to move about, "as a roaring lion, walketh about seeking whom he may devour" (I Peter 5:8). Satan is not in Hell, though that terrible place is especially for him and his angels (Matt. 25:41), and he will surely be cast into the lake of fire (Rev. 20:10); his scene of action during this age is mainly in the heavenly realms, where he has access to God and accuses the saints before Him day and night (Job 1:6-12; Rev. 12:10). His casting out of Heaven (Rev. 12:9) is still future. When Satan finally reaches Hell (the lake of fire), he will suffer eternal torment there (Rev. 20:10), though meanwhile he is a great ruler, the prince of the power of the air (Eph. 2:2), and the ruler of an innumerable host of wicked spirits in the heavenly realms (Eph. 6:12); while neither omnipresent, omnipotent, nor omniscient, through this host of wicked spirits he is able at all times to keep in touch with man and man's affairs throughout the whole world. He is also god of this age (II Cor. 4:4) and world-system (John 12:31; 14:30), which is enforced by the military forces of the world, and based upon greed, power and the love of power, selfishness, and personal pleasure. God committed the power of death to Satan, but the Lord Jesus broke that power upon the cross (Heb. 2:14, 15; Rev. 1:18). In the end times Satan will be bound for the one thousand years of the Millennium, when Christ returns to the earth; afterward he will be loosed for a "little season" (Rev. 20:1-3, 7), during which "little season" he will instigate a last rebellion against God; then, crushingly defeated, his final doom will be eternal torment, forever and ever, in the lake of fire (Rev. 20:10).

DEMONS (Devils, A.V.)—Reference is constantly being made to these beings in the New Testament. They are the emissaries of Satan in all of his projects and undertakings, and will participate in his final doom in the lake of fire (Matt. 25:41; Rev. 20:10). That they are real personalities the Scriptures many times attest, but furnish no information concerning their origin; they are not the same as the fallen angels of Jude 6 and II Peter 2:4. Their hosts are so innumerable as to almost give Satan the power of omnipresence (Mark 5:9). Many instances of their ability to enter and control men and beasts are recorded in the New Testament (Mark 5:1-14; Luke 11:14); they continually seek entrance into the bodies of God's creatures, otherwise being seemingly impotent for evil (Luke 11:24, 26); also many instances of demon possession are to be found: Matthew 4:24; 8:16, 28, 33; 9:32; 12:22; Mark 1:32; 5:18; Luke 8:36; Acts 8:7; 16:16.

Demons recognized Christ as "Most High God," and also His divine power (Matt. 8:31, 32; Mark 1:24; Acts 19:15). They realize their doom to be eternal torment (Matt. 8:29; Luke 8:31). They are capable of imposing physical diseases (Matt. 17:15-18), and are foul, unclean, baleful, fierce and hateful (Matt. 8:28; Mark 1:23; 5:3, 5; 9:17-20; Luke 6:18; 9:39). Departure from the faith (apostasy) may be caused by demon influence (I Tim. 4:1-3), also such degeneracy as is pictured in II Peter 2:10-12. Demons conduct a continual contest with believers (Eph. 6:12; I Tim. 4:1-3), but Scripture apparently denies that believers can become demon possessed (I John 4:4), though all unbelievers are subject to possible demon possession (Eph. 2:2). Their willingness to use the swine as an abode abundantly bespoke their opinion of their human habitation (Matt. 8:31). The believer's safety lies in prayer and the "armor of God" (Eph. 6:13-18). One of the terrific judgments of the Great Tribulation will be the eruption from the bottomless pit of countless numbers of demons (Rev. 9:1-11).

ANGELS—Angel (messenger) is sometimes employed of God (Gen. 16:1-13; 21:17-19; 22:11-16); of men (Luke 7:24; James 2:25; Rev. 1:20; 2:1, 8, 12, 18; 3:1, 7, 14); and of departed spirits of men (Matt. 18:10; Acts 12:15). Angels are a distinct created order of heavenly beings, above the sphere of man (Ps. 8:5; Heb. 2:7; Rev. 5:11; 7:11). Angels, being spirits (Ps. 104:4; Heb. 1:14) are invisible; but when seen of men they have been given power to assume human form (Matt. 1:20; 28:2-5; Luke 1:26-28; John 20:12; Acts 12:7, 8); they are always spoken of as masculine and would seem to be sexless (Matt. 22:30; Mark 12:25). Of their ministry Scripture states: they were present at the Creation (Job 38:7); at the giving of the law (Gal. 3:19; Acts 7:53); at Christ's birth (Luke 2:13); at Christ's temptation by Satan (Matt. 4:11); in the garden of Gethsemane (Luke 22:43); at His resurrection (Matt. 28:2); at Christ's ascension (Acts 1:10); and will appear at Christ's second coming (Matt. 24:31; 25:31; II Thess. 1:7). They are sent forth as ministering spirits to the heirs of salvation, for the physical wellbeing of believers (Ps. 34:7; 91:11; Heb. 1:14), apparently from childhood on through life (Matt. 18:10). Angels are observers and witnesses of humans (I Cor. 4:9; 11:10; I Tim. 3:16; I Peter 1:12; Luke 15:10). In the human sphere, Christ was for a little while made lower than the angels (Heb. 2:9), but now is seated far above the angels (Eph. 1:20, 21). Only two angels are mentioned by name in Scripture: the archangel Michael, related especially to Israel (Dan. 10:13, 21; 12:1, 2; Jude 9), and to have a part in the resurrection

(I Thess. 4:16); Gabriel, who has been entrusted with many heavenly messages (Dan. 8:16; 9:21; Luke 1:19, 26).

Of the fallen angels, some are unrestrained and some are bound, the latter being reserved in chains until judgment (II Peter 2:4; Jude 6; I Cor. 6:3). The former are the demons (devils, A.V.) constantly alluded to in the New Testament, and ruled by Satan, whose final doom is the lake of fire (Matt. 25:41; Rev. 20:10).

HEAVEN—Very little is revealed in the Bible concerning Heaven and the heavenly state. However, Heaven is a place, a place of joy and gladness for all who go there; the Lord Jesus said, "I go to prepare a place for you" (John 14:2, 3), and that where He is we shall be also. It is necessary that Heaven be a place, for there our Lord, in His resurrected body, sits upon a real throne beside His Father, in the highest of the heavens, far above all other heavens (Eph. 4:10). Paul was caught up into that realm, and on account of the abundance of revelations to him, he had to be given a thorn in the flesh to keep him from being too puffed up (II Cor. 12:7). Saints who have passed through death are now consciously in Heaven with God, although not yet in their resurrected bodies (II Cor. 5:1-8). Their mortal bodies remain in the graves until the rapture (I Cor. 15). But they are not unclothed or naked; nor are they floating around as invisible spirits, incapable of speech or action; neither are they asleep or unconscious. In Revelation 6:9-11 there is mention of the souls of the slain martyrs; they were seen, they were heard, they spoke, and white robes were given them. A vast number of angels will be in Heaven, an entirely separate and distinct order of beings from man; these beings are always spoken of in the masculine gender; sex, in the human sense, is never ascribed to them; neither will there be any sex among the glorified saints in Heaven, for it is written in Matthew 22:30

41

that "in the resurrection they neither marry, nor are given in marriage, but are as the angels of God in heaven." (See also Mark 12:25; Luke 20:34, 36.) We may confidently expect to know every person in Heaven—all will be our friends and "loved ones"! All this is mystery, yet true.

SAINTS—A saint is a sanctified one, one set apart for God, not a sinless person (as many erroneously think). "The sanctified," not the sinless; "saints," not those absolutely holy. "To them that are sanctified in Christ Jesus, called saints" (I Cor. 1:2). When one is saved, that very moment God separated him from the world under judgment, and set him apart unto Himself in Christ Jesus; and that instant he became a saint, that instant he was sanctified, and that sanctification is a perfect one: "He hath perfected forever them that are sanctified" (Heb. 10:14).

Christians are saints; they are not called to become saints, they become saints instantaneously at their new birth. This fact is set forth everywhere in the New Testament, and yet there is much confusion among the translators. We do not become saints by acting in a saintly way, but because we are constituted saints we should manifest saintliness; undoubtedly we are called upon to live "as becometh saints" (Rom. 16:2); but it is highly important to see that if we have received the gift of eternal life through Jesus Christ our Lord, we are already saints, sanctified ones, set apart for Him, belonging to Him, saints by His own designation, His own calling; *called saints*—not "called to be saints" but *called saints*, meaning "saints by calling." Saints in the same way that Paul was an apostle (Rom. 1:1, 2), by divine call. Finally, only God can make a saint, not the human heads of an earthly church.

APOSTLE—Apostle (one sent forth) is the designation of the Twelve (Matt. 10:2-4) called by the Lord Jesus Christ during His public life; of Paul, also called by the Lord Jesus after His ascension (Rom. 1:1; I Cor. 9:1, 2); of Barnabas, set apart by the Holy Spirit (Acts 13:2), and thereafter called an apostle (Acts 14:14); of Matthias, selected by casting lots to assume the place left vacant by Judas Iscariot (Acts 1: 16-26).

The apostles were successively chosen by Jesus for the purpose of being eyewitnesses to the events of His life, and to testify to mankind concerning Him (Matt. 10:2-42); but primarily as eyewitnesses of His resurrection (Acts 1:22; I Cor. 9:1). Another badge of office was their power of working miracles, given them by the Lord Jesus or the Holy Spirit (Matt. 10:1; Acts 5:15, 16; 16:16-18; 28:8, 9). They were charged with announcing to Israel only (Matt. 10:5, 6) the kingdom of Heaven as at hand (Matt. 10:7), to heal the sick and raise the dead (Matt. 10:8). One of them, Peter, received the keys of the kingdom (Matt. 16:19), with which he subsequently opened the kingdom to Jew and Gentile. The apostleship was later endued with the baptism of the Holy Spirit (Acts 2:1-4), and given the power to bestow the Holy Spirit to believers by the laying on of hands (Acts 8:18). It became the privilege of the apostles to become the foundation of the whole structure of the new temple (Eph. 2:20-22), and to preach the good news of salvation to the whole civilized world, both Jews and Gentiles. The Lord Jesus Himself was termed the Apostle and High Priest of our confession (Heb. 3:1).

TIMES OF THE GENTILES—The times of the Gentiles (Luke 21:24) began with the Jewish captivity in Babylon under Nebuchadnezzar (Dan. 1:1, 2), and will continue until the Lord Jesus comes again in power and glory to set up His own throne from which He will rule the world during the Millennium (Rev. 19:11-21). The period of time has already extended for over twenty-five hundred years.

WORLD-SYSTEM—Greek *kosmos*, anglicized *cosmos*, meaning a system characterized by order.

Satan claimed to be ruler of the world (Matt. 4:8, 9), and this was conceded by the Lord Jesus when on earth (John 12:31; 14:30; 18:36). Satan could not conquer Him, his temptations being futile; but he goes on with the same temptations, and has succeeded astonishingly with the monstrosity which calls itself Christendom; blind, unbelieving Christendom attempts to rule the world, to be on the throne, basing her principles upon a foundation subtly furnished by Satan—greed, power, world-conquest, selfishness, pleasure. The world-system as set up by Christendom is impressive—intellectual, externally religious, learned, cultured, but agitated with national and business competitions, enforced by armies and navies, and dominated over all by its real ruler, Satan.

FULFILLED PROPHECY—Fulfilled prophecy (II Peter 1:19-21) is a proof of inspiration because the Scripture predictions of future events were uttered so long before the events transpired that no merely human sagacity or foresight could have anticipated them. These predictions are so detailed, minute, and specific as to exclude the possibility that they were fortunate guesses. Hundreds of predictions concerning Israel, the land of Canaan, Babylon, Assyria, Egypt, and numerous personages, so ancient, so singular, so seemingly improbable, as well as so detailed and definite that no mortal could have anticipated them, have been fulfilled by the elements, and by men who were ignorant of them, or who utterly disbelieved them, or who struggled with frantic desperation to avoid their fulfillment. It is certain, therefore, that the Scriptures which contain them are inspired. "Prophecy came not in olden time by the will of man; but holy men of God spake as they were moved by the Holy Ghost" (II Peter 1:21).

THE SEVEN DISPENSATIONS—A dispensation is a time of trial or testing for the human race, relative to the submission to and acceptance of a definite disclosure of God Himself or of His will. Scripture reveals seven such dispensations.

(1) Innocence, lasting from the creation of man to his expulsion from Eden (Gen. 3:23, 24). Man was created in perfect innocence, given an ideal location in which to live, and cautioned as to the results of sin. Eve, the woman, then succumbed to Satan's tempting, an appeal to her pride (Gen. 3:5, 6), but Adam deliberately, of his own volition (I Tim. 2:14).

(2) Conscience, lasting from the expulsion from the garden to the Flood. Man by disobeying God obtained a knowledge of good and evil (Gen. 3:5, 7), which brought the human conscience into being. Governed by conscience, man failed dismally, with results as God saw in Genesis 6:5.

(3) Human government, which, beginning at the Flood, is still going on. Under God's covenant with Noah, human government was established (Gen. 9:1-6), a new test for man, and Jew and Gentile became responsible to govern; the Jews until Israel, failing signally under the Palestinian Covenant (Deut. 28; 29; 30:1-10), began the period of the captivities, and world government then became the obligation of the Gentiles alone (Luke 21:24; Acts 15:14-17), until the "times of the Gentiles be fulfilled." The test of rule by the races terminated with the confusion of tongues (Babel); that of rule by the Jews with the captivities, and the test of rule by the Gentiles will terminate with the coming of the Lord Jesus Christ in power and glory (Rev. 19:11-21).

(4) Promise, beginning with the Abrahamic covenant which is still in force, and will be consummated when Christ again comes to the earth, and extending to the accepting of the law by Israel (Exod. 19:8). Grace was the basis of this test, with Moses as the deliverer, bringing the children of Israel, through divine power, out of bondage to Egypt (Exod. 19:4). But Israel failed by discarding grace for the law (Exod. 19:8), and the dispensation ended.

(5) Law, lasting from Sinai to the cross of Calvary (Gal. 3:19-25). This test as a nation ended with the captivities, but the dispensation of law itself extended to the cross, the time in the promised land being one long continuation of sin, and breaking of the law.

(6) Grace, beginning with Calvary and extending to the Rapture of the Church. The test is belief on the Lord Jesus Christ (John 1:12, 13; 3:16; 3:36; I John 5:1-13). Jew and Gentile alike failed the test, rejecting and crucifying the Son of God (Acts 4:27), and for over nineteen hundred years believers have been awaiting His return, the descent into the air for His Church (I Thess. 4:13-18), which will end the dispensation of grace.

(7) The fullness of times, or kingdom age (Eph. 1:10), beginning with Christ's second advent, and extending for one thousand years—the millennial period. This is the kingdom promised to David (Luke 1:31-33), over which the Lord Jesus Christ, as the only rightful heir, will reign. Only righteousness will prevail when Christ takes this throne (Isa. 11:3-5), and in that day He will judge the world in righteousness (Acts 17:31); He will repay with tribulation those who afflict the righteous (II Thess. 1:6, 7); He will recompense the times of suffering with glory (Rom. 8:17, 18); He will take away the blindness from Israel, and restore them to godliness in the Beloved (Rom. 11:25-27); He will end the times of the Gentiles, and establish His throne in

the kingdom, when He smites the nations and rules them with a rod of iron (Rev. 19:15-21); He will terminate this seventh and last dispensation by delivering the kingdom to God the Father, having destroyed every rule, every authority and every power; for He must reign until He puts all enemies under His feet (I Cor. 15:24, 25).

THE EIGHT COVENANTS—(1) The Edenic Covenant (Gen. 1:26-31); a conditional covenant which God made with Adam, depending on the faithfulness of Adam, who failed in the Fall.

(2) The Adamic Covenant (Gen. 3:14-19); an unconditional where God tells man his lot in life on account of his sin, with the promise of a Redeemer.

(3) The Noahic Covenant (Gen. 9:1-18); an unconditional covenant, giving authority for human government on the earth and promising no recurrence of the Flood.

(4) The Abrahamic Covenant (Gen. 15:18); unconditional and promising the founding of the nation Israel, which God also confirmed to Isaac and Jacob (Gen. 26:24; 35:12), reaffirming the promise of redemption.

(5) The Mosaic Covenant (Exod. 20:1—31:18); a conditional covenant with Israel, dividing the law into the commandments (Exod. 20:1-17); the judgments (Exod. 21:1—24:11); and the ordinances (Exod. 24:12—31:18). The conditions may be termed: "I will if ye will, I will not if ye will not." Israel's failure was predicted by God (Deut. 28:63-68), but since the cross no believer has been under the law (Rom. 6:14).

(6) The Palestinian Covenant (Deut. 30:1-10); an unconditional covenant, looking forward to the final possession of the promised land by Israel. Deuteronomy 28, 29 is actually a part of this covenant.

(7) The Davidic Covenant (II Sam. 7:4-16); uncondi-

tional, and promising David an unending royal lineage, throne and kingdom, to endure forever. The Lord Jesus Christ is the last of the royal line (Matt. 1:1; Rom. 1:3), the only heir, and will yet sit upon that throne (Luke 1:31-33), fulfilling the promise to David.

(8) The New Covenant (Mark 14:24; Luke 22:20; Heb. 8:6; 10:16); made in His blood, and unconditional, the covenant of divine grace, guaranteeing all of God's promises to man, based upon the shed blood of Jesus Christ, and securing the eternal blessings, under the Abrahamic Covenant, of all believers.

THE NEW COVENANT—The New Covenant is clearly defined in Jeremiah 31:31-34, where, of course, its direct application is to Israel, the fulfillment awaiting a time yet future for the nation. But the language of Jeremiah 31 is quoted in Hebrews 10:16, 17, where it is shown by the context that all who have believed on Christ, Jews or Gentiles, have entered into the blessing of the New Covenant, based upon the offering of the body of Jesus Christ "once for all" (v. 10), by which "offering he hath perfected forever them that are sanctified" (v. 14). The fact that it is necessary to believe on Christ in order to be saved does not constitute a *condition* of this covenant, but this belief is rather the *basis of admission* into its eternal blessings. The covenant is not related to the unsaved, but is made with all those who believe, promising the faithfulness of God in their behalf.

THE VIRGIN BIRTH—The virgin birth of the Lord Jesus Christ was demanded by the Old Testament Scriptures (Isa. 7:14), and declared by the New Testament (Matt. 1:18-25). He could not be the natural son of Joseph, as He then would be cut off from all right to the throne of David, for Joseph was of the seed of Coniah; God declared in Jeremiah 22:24-30 that no descendant of Coniah could ever sit upon that throne. The genealogy of Joseph in Matthew 1 shows him to be descended from Jechonias (another form of Coniah's name), while Luke 3 shows that through His mother Mary the Lord Jesus descended from David, not through Solomon and Coniah, but through another son of David named Nathan. No one is a Christian who denies our Lord's virgin birth.

THE LORD JESUS CHRIST—Christ (Greek *Christos*, anointed), the Greek form of the Hebrew "Messiah" (Dan. 9:25, 26), is the official name of our Lord, as Jesus is His human name (Luke 1:31; 2:21). The name or title "Christ" connects Him with the entire Old Testament foreview (Zech. 12:8) of a coming prophet (Deut. 18:15-19), priest (Ps. 110:4), and king (II Sam. 7:7-10). As these were typically anointed with oil (I Kings 19:16; Exod. 29:7; I Sam. 16:13), so Jesus was anointed with the Holy Spirit (Matt. 3:16; Mark 1:10, 11; Luke 3:21, 22; John 1:32, 33), thus becoming officially "the Christ." Hence His full and complete name is the "Lord Jesus Christ," and thus used it is the fullest reverence.

THE TWO ADVENTS OF CHRIST—That the Old Testament prophets were perplexed by their own prophecies, and unable to distinguish between the two advents of the Messiah is clear from I Peter 1:10, 11. According to Old Testament prophecy Christ is shown coming as a gentle lamb, led to the slaughter (Isa. 53:1-12), and as a glorious conqueror, the Lion of the tribe of Judah (Isa. 11:1-12; Jer. 23:5, 6); at times the two aspects mingle so completely in one passage that the prophets were puzzled at the apparent contradiction. This was, of course, God's way of keeping secret in His own counsels the coming events of this present

49

age. However, ultimately the mystery was cleared up by being fulfilled in part: Messiah, the Lord Jesus Christ, was born of the Virgin, as Isaiah had prophesied (Isa. 7:14), and commenced His ministry among men, announcing the kingdom of Heaven as being "at hand" (Matt. 4:17).

Old Testament prophecy was to the effect that Messiah should be born of a virgin, of the tribe of Judah (Gen. 49:10), and of the house of David (Isa. 11:1; Jer. 33:21); was to die a death of sacrifice (Isa. 53:1-12), crucified (Ps. 22:1-21); be resurrected from the dead (Ps. 16:8-11), and return to earth in a second coming (Deut. 30:3). These prophecies, except for His coming again, have all been perfectly fulfilled by the Lord Jesus Christ, such as no other could possibly do, and this predicted return is one of the most important themes of the New Testament; there it is shown to be a real happening, bodily, personal (Matt. 24:30; Mark 14:62; Luke 17:24; John 14:3; Acts 1:11; I Thess. 4:14-18); apparently the very first event of unfulfilled prophecy next to take place will be the Lord's descent into the air for His Church, when the dead in Christ will rise, together with all living believers, to meet Him in the air (I Thess. 4:14-18). Then after the Great Tribulation He will return to earth together with all His saints, to set up His throne for the thousand years of the kingdom age.

THE SECOND COMING OF CHRIST—The second coming of the Lord Jesus Christ begins with the Rapture of the Church in the air, followed by the Great Tribulation, during which time will also occur the judgments at the judgment seat of Christ, which constitute the giving of rewards for good works, consummating in His coming to the earth in power and great glory; the elapsed time for these momentous events will be at least seven years, the period of Daniel's seventieth week (Dan. 9:27), which corresponds to the time of the Great Tribulation (Matt. 24:29, 30).

1. The word Rapture is nowhere found in Scripture; it is a word used to designate an event, and comes from a root meaning "to be caught up." The Rapture, Christ's descent into the air to meet His caught-up Church, constituting every believer both living and dead, is the next event of divine prophecy to take place; there is no known prophecy yet unfulfilled between the present time and this tremendous event, so marvelously and concisely pictured by the apostle Paul in I Thessalonians 4:13-18:

> But I would not have you to be ignorant, brethren, concerning them which are asleep, that ye sorrow not, even as others which have no hope. For if we believe that Jesus died and rose again, even so them also which sleep in Jesus will God bring with him. For this we say unto you by the word of the Lord, that we which are alive and remain unto the coming of the Lord will not precede them which are asleep. For the Lord Himself shall descend from heaven with a shout, with the voice of the archangel, and with the trump of God: and the dead in Christ shall rise first: then we which are alive and remain shall be caught up together with them in the clouds, to meet the Lord in the air: and so shall we ever be with the Lord. Wherefore comfort one another with these words.

2. Following the Rapture, Christ sets up His judgment seat, probably somewhere in the air, before which all His saints will appear one by one (Rom. 14:10; II Cor. 5:9, 10), for the judgment of their works, and the giving of promised rewards (I Cor. 3:11-15; 4:5). This will transpire in all probability during the seven years of the Great Tribulation on the earth.

3. After completion of the giving of His rewards, in Reve-

lation 19:11-16, the Lord Jesus Christ is seen as He is leaving Heaven with His saints and angels, for the purpose of destroying His enemies, and setting up the kingdom of Heaven on the earth:

And I saw heaven opened, and behold a white horse: and he that sat upon him was called Faithful and True, and in righteousness he doth judge and make war. His eyes were as a flame of fire, and on his head were many crowns; and he had a name written, that no man knew, but he himself. And he was clothed with a vesture dipped in blood: and his name is called The Word of God. And the armies which were in heaven followed him upon white horses, clothed in fine linen, white and clean. And out of his mouth goeth a sharp sword, that with it he should smite the nations: and he shall rule them with a rod of iron: and he treadeth the winepress of the fierceness and wrath of Almighty God. And he hath on his vesture and on his thigh a name written, KING OF KINGS AND LORD OF LORDS.

In chapter 24 of Matthew He is seen again:
For as the lightning cometh out of the east, and shineth even unto the west; so shall the coming of the Son of man be. . . Immediately after the tribulation of those days shall the sun be darkened, and the moon shall not give her light, and the stars shall fall from heaven, and the powers of the heavens shall be shaken: and then shall appear the sign of the Son of man in heaven: and then shall all the tribes of the earth mourn, and they shall see the Son of man coming in the clouds of heaven with power and great glory.
(See also Isa. 2:12-21; 13:9-13; Zech. 2:10-13; Luke 17:28-30; 21:25-27.)

And so, with power and great glory, He returns to the

earth, establishing His throne, upon which He reigns, together with His saints for a thousand years (Rev. 20:4-6); after which the kingdom is turned over to God the Father.

CHRIST THE ROCK—Moses, at God's direction, smote the rock that the people might drink (Exod. 17:6); the rock was a type of Christ who was smitten (crucified) that all who will may drink of the life that flows from Him (I Cor. 10:4; John 4:13, 14; 7:37-39). Christ is also that foundation rock and chief cornerstone of the Church (Eph. 2:20); but the "rock of offense and stumblingstone" to the Jews (Rom. 9:32, 33; I Cor. 1:23), though He will yet be the "headstone" to Israel as a nation (Zech. 4:7). He is that "stone cut out without hands" which smote the feet of the image (Gentile power) and broke them to pieces (Dan. 2:34). He will be the stone of Matthew 21:44, which will grind the wicked to powder.

THE LAW OF CHRIST—The new commandment, given by Jesus, is the law of divine love, "that ye love one another, as I have loved you" (John 13:34). It is that "law of liberty" of James 1:25; 2:12, the "bearing of another's burdens" of Galatians 6:2, the "loving with a pure heart" of I Peter 1:22, 23, outpouring without restraint in the power of the Spirit, that law of the heart and mind (Heb. 10:16), of the new covenant of grace.

PROPHET, PRIEST AND KING—**Jesus the Prophet**—Our Lord exercised His prophetic office when He was here on earth, telling forth the message of God. This He did not only by His words, but also by His acts and in His own person. Moses predicted (Deut. 18:15, 17-19), about one thousand four hundred and fifty years before the birth of Jesus of Nazareth, that sometime in the future God would raise up for Israel from among their own race a perfect and inerrant Prophet into whose mouth God would put His own words, and who should speak all that God commanded Him. Almost fifteen hundred years later, some thirty years after the birth of Jesus of Nazareth, Peter (Acts 3:22, 23), after he was filled with the Holy Spirit and so qualified to speak for God, declared that the prophecy made through Moses had been fulfilled in Jesus of Nazareth. A prophet is one who speaks not his own words but the words he receives from God as he speaks; he is not only one who foretells, but one who forthtells as well. The Lord Jesus Himself claimed that He was such a Prophet (John 7:16; 8:28; 12:49, 50; 14:24).

Prediction constituted a large part of what the Lord Jesus said as the mouthpiece of God the Father, and among His fulfilled predictions are the following:

1. His prediction of His own death and resurrection in the exact manner of their happening (John 2:19; Matt. 16:21; 20:18, 19).

2. He predicted a great outward growth of His kingdom, and simultaneously a thorough corruption of its inward life and doctrine, which is seen in the twin parables of the mustard seed and the leaven (Matt. 13:31-33).

3. He predicted the destruction of Jerusalem, describing its character and details forty years before it happened (Matt. 24:1, 2; Luke 19:41-44). When Jesus made these predictions, about A.D. 30, there seemed no possibility of their fulfillment; yet they were fulfilled to the very letter when Jerusalem was visited with the siege of agony and destruction by the Romans under Titus in A.D. 70, such as was never visited upon any other city.

4. He predicted the centuries-long subjection of Jerusalem and the Jew to Gentile domination, to be ended only when the times of the Gentiles were fulfilled (Luke 21:20-24).

Over nineteen centuries of history have confirmed the truth and literal accuracy of the first part of this prediction. We are surely on the eve of the fulfillment of the second part, when the times of the Gentiles "shall be fulfilled."

5. He predicted that the Jews, for centuries scattered over the whole earth and subjected to terrible persecutions, would preserve their race identity until He should come to deliver them (Matt. 24:34; Mark 13:30; Luke 21:32); in these three passages the word translated "generation" refers to "race," meaning the Jewish race. Centuries have passed, but the Jew is still a Jew.

6. He predicted imperishableness for His words, not only among the wrecks of philosophies, religions, kingdoms and empires, but even in the passing away of Heaven and earth (Matt. 24:35).

The following are among the unfulfilled predictions of the Lord Jesus:

1. The most important, He is coming again (John 14:1-3; I Thess. 4:16-18).

2. He predicted that the time of His second coming will be a time when human society is totally absorbed in worldly pursuits, profiteering, pleasure-seeking, and reeking in sin (Luke 17:26-30; 21:35; Matt. 24:44). Surely this is applicable to the present time!

3. He predicted that the time immediately preceding His coming will be a time when human society is totally unsettled in its politics and business, with its international affairs in utter confusion (Luke 21:25-27). Then He said: "But when these things begin to come to pass, then look up, and lift up your heads; because your redemption draweth nigh" (Luke 21:28).

4. He predicted that as a result of His coming, He is to take the reins of government, that all the evils of society are to be corrected, and that there is to be a reign of universal

righteousness throughout the world (Matt. 19:28-30; 25: 31, 32, 34, 46). All the brightest and loftiest dreams of the world's best poets and social philosophers will be more than realized then, when His words find their fulfillment in His own personal return to this earth. Even so, come, Lord Jesus!

Jesus the Priest—The Lord Jesus is now exercising His priestly office as He ministers at the right hand of the Majesty on high, making intercession for His people.

A true priest, as is evident from a study of both the Old Testament and the New Testament use of the word, is one who represents sinful people before a holy God; one who makes it possible for penitent sinners to stand in God's holy presence and to have joyous communion with Him. The priest represents God's people before God and makes communion with God possible in two ways:

1. By making propitiation for their sins (Heb. 2:17, R.V.). This the Lord Jesus did by the sacrifice on Calvary of Himself, once for all, and by the offering of His shed blood. "But he, when he had offered one sacrifice for sins forever, sat down on the right hand of God" (Heb. 10:12).

2. The priest represents the redeemed people of God before God by interceding for them (Heb. 7:23-25). In two points of much importance our High Priest, Jesus, excels all other priests: (a) they were hindered by death from continuing, whereas Jesus "ever liveth" to make intercession; (b) the old Aaronic priesthood was permitted in the holy of holies but once a year, while our High Priest, Jesus, is in the true holy of holies, Heaven itself, forever.

The characteristics of our great High Priest are:

1. He is a Priest by divine appointment (Heb. 5:6).
2. He is a perfect Priest in moral character (Heb. 7:26-28).
3. He is a merciful and faithful High Priest (Heb. 2:17).

4. He is a sympathetic High Priest (Heb. 4:14-16).

5. He is an everlasting Priest (Heb. 7:23-25).

Jesus, our High Priest, has made perfect atonement for our sins forever; therefore there is no cloud between God and the believer in Christ, no matter how many, or how great, the believer's sins may have been; and He is in God's presence today, now and forever, to intercede for us; He knows all of Satan's wiles and can save us from falling Satan's prey; He can also take up our case if we do fall. As the apostle John puts it (I John 2:1): "If any man sin, we [believers in Christ] have an advocate with the Father, Jesus Christ the righteous."

Jesus the King—The Lord Jesus will show Himself at His second coming, not just as King, but in His royal and regal character, "the blessed and only Sovereign, the King of kings and Lord of lords" (I Tim. 6:15, R.S.V.). Now God has a great deal to say in His Book about Jesus the Prophet; He has a great deal to say in His Book about Jesus the Priest; but God has a great deal more to say in His Book about Jesus the King.

Where will He reign?

1. He is to reign on earth (Ps. 72:7, 8; Jer. 23:5; Dan. 7:13, 14; Rev. 19:11-16). His kingdom, it is clear, will not be a heavenly kingdom, but an earthly kingdom—heavenly in character, but on the earth; therefore it is called "Kingdom of heaven," that is, the kingdom of heavenly character existing on the earth.

2. Jerusalem is to be the center of His reign (Ps. 2:6). Zion is mentioned in the Bible some one hundred and fifty times, and always refers to Jerusalem; Jerusalem then is to be the seat, the throne city, of Jesus the King.

3. The extent of His kingdom will be the whole earth (Ps. 72:6-11; Isa. 2:2, 3; Dan. 7:13, 14; Zech. 8:20-23).

When will He reign?

His reign will begin when Israel's sorrows culminate in the Great Tribulation that is coming, and He comes to deliver His people (Rev. 19:11-16; Jer. 23:5, 6; Zech. 14:1-4, 9).

What will be the character of His reign?

1. His reign will be one of absolute righteousness and justice (Ps. 72:2-7; Isa. 11:9).

2. His reign will be one of universal, everlasting peace (Isa. 2:4; Micah 4:2, 3).

3. His reign will be one of universal plenty (Micah 4:4-7). All the Utopian dreams will be realized when He is King.

4. His reign will have a special regard for the rights and interests of the poor and oppressed (Ps. 72:2, 4, 12-14).

5. His reign will be world-wide (Ps. 72:6-8).

6. His reign will be one of glory (Ps. 72:17-19).

7. His reign will be everlasting (Dan. 7:13, 14; Luke 1:32, 33; Rev. 11:15).

His millennial reign will terminate with the end of the thousand years, when the Great White Throne comes into view, and the last enemy, death, is abolished (I Cor. 15:26); then He delivers up the kingdom to the Father (I Cor. 15:24); but of Jesus' kingdom there shall be no end (Luke 1:33); "he shall reign forever and ever" (Rev. 11:15); so then *the eternal reign* of the Lord Jesus commences, in eternal subordination to the Father, "that God may be all in all" (I Cor. 15:28); or as it is in the Revised Standard Version, "that God may be everything to everyone."

Even so, come, Lord Jesus!

THE CRUCIFIXION—WHICH DAY OF THE WEEK?—There is a great deal of evidence that our Lord was crucified on Wednesday, not on Friday. The impression that the crucifixion occurred on Friday is due to the fact that it took place on the *day before the Sabbath*, and it has been generally assumed that the Sabbath referred to was the weekly Sabbath, which fell on Saturday; however there were many sabbaths in the Hebrew calendar besides the fifty-two weekly Sabbaths, and the Sabbaths by which the feast of the Passover and unleavened bread was begun and ended were counted as peculiarly sacred Sabbaths. The Passover always fell on the fourteenth of the Hebrew month Abib (Lev. 23:5), and of course would be on a different day of the week each year. The evidence on the subject of our Lord's crucifixion leads this author to the conclusion that the feast began that year on Thursday—and "that sabbath day was an high day" (John 19:31)—and that the crucifixion was on the day before, which would be Wednesday.

The Jewish day began at six in the evening instead of at midnight. The body of our Lord was placed in the tomb just before six on Wednesday evening, which was the beginning of Thursday; it remained there through Thursday (night and day), Friday (night and day), and Saturday (night and day), and was raised from the dead just as Sunday was beginning (Matt. 28:1), or what we now call Saturday evening about six o'clock. Thus the entombment was endured through three days and three nights, fulfilling our Lord's own prediction in Matthew 12:40. No one saw our Lord's resurrection, and the record shows that when the disciples visited the tomb immediately after the weekly Sabbath had ended, that is, on Saturday night, they found the tomb empty.

THE TRANSFIGURATION SCENE—The transfiguration scene (Matt. 17:1-9) is a representation in type of the coming kingdom in all its fullness, and fulfilled our Lord's words as recorded in Matthew 16:28. On the mount were (a) the Lord Jesus Himself in His glorified body (Matt. 17:2); (b) Moses, in his glorified body, and depicting all the saved who enter the kingdom through death; (c) Elijah, also in his glorified body, depicting all the saved who enter the kingdom by translation. (See I Cor. 15:50-53 and I Thess. 4:13-18.) (d) Peter, James, and John in their natural bodies of the flesh, depicting Israel in the coming kingdom, and (e) the multitude of people left at the mountain's base, also in their natural bodies, depicting the Gentile nations who are finally taken into the kingdom for the Millennium (Isa. 11:10-12). That the apostle Peter realized these things he makes very clear in the first chapter of his second epistle.

THE SON OF MAN—This title was adopted by our Lord, and He applied it to Himself in the four Gospels seventy-eight times. It was His earthly title as representative of the human race in the same sense that Son of David is His Jewish title, and Son of God His divine, or heavenly title. Son of Man, Son of David, Son of God—all combined in the same Person. But the title of Son of Man took Him on beyond the Jews, and, in fact, should show to the world that His purpose in death, resurrection, and return to the earth is for the redemption of the human race (Luke 19:10), to all who believe (Luke 12:8). When He uses that title "Son of Man" He has in mind the day when He shall return to the whole human race (Matt. 24:30). It was not a title to show that He had a fellow feeling for man and was brother to all, nor to denote that He was not divine, for He repeatedly asserted His deity (Luke 5:24); but was a title that could not be used against Him by His enemies. It fulfilled in Him the Old Testament prediction of a coming Deliverer (Gen. 3:15; 12:3).

THE LORD'S SUPPER—This name was given by Paul to the commemorative ordinance instituted by our Lord on the evening preceding His crucifixion (I Cor. 11:20). Paul's

60

account is the earliest record of the institution of the Supper probably early in A.D. 57, just twenty-seven years after the Supper was instituted. The apostle had introduced it five years earlier, when he organized the Corinthian church and "delivered" to them the ordinance (v. 23). He pledges his own truthfulness and authority for the correctness of his account by saying "I received" and "I delivered." He refers to the source of his information: he had not been an eye-witness to the event; he had not been present at the institution of the Supper; but he had received from the Lord what he had delivered to them.

These words are capable of two interpretations: either Paul had been granted a special communication direct from the risen Lord, or else he had received the account from the Lord through the Lord's apostles, participants in the first Supper. Matthew, an eyewitness, and Mark, the companion of Peter, who was present at the institution of the Supper, also record the circumstances; so does Paul's companion, Luke. Wishing to fulfill all righteousness and to honor the ceremonial law while it continued, Jesus made arrangements to eat the Pass-over with His disciples (Matt. 26:17-19). Since the paschal lamb was killed in the evening, the paschal feast necessarily took place in the evening (Matt. 26:20). Wine mixed with water had come into use on such occasions. When, therefore, our Lord was about to follow up the Supper by the Com-munion, there was wine mixed with water on the table. So also was there unleavened bread. He and His disciples were sitting (Matt. 26:20), by which is meant that, after the cus-tom of the time, they half sat, half reclined on couches. When the paschal feast was finished, Jesus took bread and blessed it, at the same time rendering thanks for it; giving it to His disciples, He said: "This is my body which is given for you; this do in remembrance of me." And the cup in like man-ner after supper saying: "This cup is the new covenant in my blood, even that which is poured out for you" (Luke 22:19, 20, R.V.), "which is shed for many unto remission of sins" (Matt. 26:28, R.V.). The object for which the Lord's Supper was instituted was to keep Him in remembrance (Luke 22:19). It was to show forth "the Lord's death till he come" (I Cor. 11:25, 26). The feast was not confined to the apostles or to the Jewish Christians, but was celebrated in the churches of the Gentiles also, for instance at Corinth (I Cor. 10:15-21). It was understood to be the privilege of the Church for all time. The table on which the bread was placed was known as the Lord's table (I Cor. 10:21); the cup as the cup of blessing (v. 16), and was also called the cup of the Lord (I Cor. 10:21; 11:27).

THE SEVEN SPIRITS OF GOD—There is, of course, but one Holy Spirit. Seven, however, is the number of spiritual or mystical completeness, and the figure, therefore, implies the fullness of the Holy Spirit, that is, the one Spirit in the sevenfold plenitude of His power. This is clearly indicated in Isaiah 11:1, 2, where we read of the Branch of the Lord, that is, the Messiah, upon whom shall rest

1. The spirit of the Lord
2. The spirit of wisdom
3. The spirit of understanding
4. The spirit of counsel
5. The spirit of might
6. The spirit of knowledge
7. The spirit of the fear of the Lord.

THE RIGHTEOUSNESS OF GOD—The righteousness of God, relating to salvation, is that righteousness which is reckoned to the believer, "even the righteousness of God which is by faith unto all and upon all them that believe" (Rom. 3:22). Christ Himself is righteousness, and is made righteousness unto all who put their trust in Him (I Cor. 1:30; II Cor. 5:21); consequently believers *are* the righteous.

THE PRAYER OF INTERCESSION—The beautiful and lovely prayer of the Lord Jesus Christ to the Father, as recorded in the Gospel of John (chap. 17), depicting the ultimate in freedom of communion between Father and Son. In this lovely prayer our Lord several times refers to believers as having been given to Him by the Father, and He makes seven requests of the Father: (1) that the Father will glorify the Son that the Son may glorify Him (v. 1); (2) that the Father will glorify the Son with the glory He had before the world was made (v. 5); (3) for the spiritual safekeeping of believers in the world (v. 11); (4) for the sanctification of believers through the truth of His Word (v. 17); (5) that as He and the Father are one, believers may be one in them (v. 21); (6) for the belief of the world (v. 21); (7) that believers may be with Him, where He is, to behold His glory (v. 24).

These spiritual benefits are given by our Lord to His followers: eternal life (v. 2); the manifestation of the Father's name (v. 6); the Father's Words of truth (vv. 8, 14); His own (Christ's) joy (v. 13); His own glory, given Him by the Father (v. 22).

This prayer may well be said to deserve far more the title of "The Lord's Prayer" than the one of Matthew 6:9-13.

PRAYER—Believers become children of God through the new birth (John 3:3, 5), which fact makes prayer both logical and sensible, for what child would hesitate to ask his father for something he wishes or needs? The Lord Jesus makes this relationship of father and son the foundation for prayer, as He gives the disciples the prayer of Matthew 6:9-13. This is the so-called "Lord's Prayer," and was given to Jewish disciples during the dispensation of law, before the Church was formed and before the present dispensation of grace had begun. It would be more properly called the "Disciples' Prayer."

There are, however, many petitions in the prayer which a Christian may properly offer. But the prayer is not in the name of Christ, which is the true basis for all Christian prayer (John 14:13, 14; 16:23-27), and it has one petition which no really instructed believer since Christ's crucifixion and resurrection can properly offer, namely, "forgive us our debts, as we forgive our debtors." This is on the principle of righteousness, but not on the principle of grace. In the Christian dispensation the Christian is already forgiven according to the riches of God's grace (Eph. 1:7; 4:32; Col. 2:13; I John 2:12), and the measure of his forgiveness from God is by no means according to the measure of his forgiveness toward others. The true principle of forgiveness under grace is stated in Ephesians 4:32: "Be ye kind one to another, tenderhearted, forgiving one another, even as God for Christ's sake hath forgiven you." The Lord's Prayer, so-called, is unquestionably not upon Church ground, but upon kingdom ground; and from our Lord's later teaching on prayer (John 16:23-27) it is seen that believers' prayers should always be addressed to the Father in the name of the Son, though it is certainly correct and according to Scripture to pray directly to the Son (I Cor. 1:2; Rom. 10:12, 13).

Strictly speaking, only believers can pray (Ps. 66:18); but the sinner, sorry for and humbled by his sins, and desiring pardon, can pray so that God will hear (Rom. 10:13). Prayer is the privilege of the Christian, who, by the grace of God, has been made a priest, to draw near to the Father in the holy of holies, to "come boldly to the throne of grace" (Heb. 4:16), and speak freely to Him in prayer in the name of the

Lord Jesus, fully expecting to receive that for which he prays, not being discouraged by delayed answers.

PEACE—Three types of peace are spoken of in Scripture: "peace with God" (Rom. 1:7; Eph. 2:14-17), which comes when believers are born again and as a result of justification by faith; (2) "peace of God" (Phil. 4:7), which is that peace of soul and spirit of all believers who, being at peace *with* God, "have no anxiety about anything" (Phil. 4:6, R.S.V.), having cast all anxieties and cares upon Him through prayer and supplication with thanksgiving; (3) "peace on earth," which is that unlimited peace promised for the world when Christ establishes His kingdom on earth (Isa. 9:6, 7; 11:1-12; Luke 2:14). All of this is most wonderful, and something of which the world knows nothing, for it all comes through our Lord Jesus Christ.

LOVE—Love for others is a desire for and a delight in their good; love is not mere fondness for others, nor pleasure in their society. The character of others may be hateful, and their society disagreeable, but still a real desire for their welfare is love (Matt. 5:43-47; I John 3:14, 16, 17).

While Christians should love *all* men, they should and will have a peculiar love for God's born-again children (Gal. 6:10; I Peter 2:17; I Thess. 3:12).

We should love our neighbor (Luke 10:29-37); we should love our enemies, the ones whom we would be least likely to love (Matt. 5:44); husbands should love their wives (Eph. 5:25), and wives their husbands (Titus 2:4).

Christ Jesus is the author of our love, and it is for His sake that we love. Our special love to the brethren is because of their special relation to Him, and so, we should love in Jesus Christ (I Cor. 16:24). We should love without hypocrisy, a genuine love, unfeigned (Rom. 12:9). Much professed love is mere pretense; much calling of one another "brother" is hollow formalism and sham. We should love not merely in word but in deed and truth; not in saying but in doing; not in professing but in practice (I John 3:18), from the heart, intensely (I Peter 1:22, R.V.).

Love is manifested by abstaining from everything that would injure another (Rom. 13:10); by doing good as we have opportunity; it is not merely negative—abstaining from doing injury, but positive, *doing good* (Gal. 6:10); by serving others, as illustrated by the Lord Jesus (John 13:1-5; Phil. 2:4-7); the man who wishes to be served, but will not serve, does not love; love seeks lowly places of service.

Love is manifested by our not seeking our own, but our neighbor's good (I Cor. 10:24, R.V.); by not looking to our own things, but to the things of others (Phil. 2:4, R.V.); by bearing each other's burdens (Gal. 6:2); bearing the infirmities of the weak, not pleasing ourselves, but pleasing others for what is good for edifying (Rom. 15:1-3, R.V.), Christ being the great example here also.

Love is manifested by forgiving and comforting the wayward (II Cor. 2:7, 8); by restoring in meekness the one overtaken in any trespass (Gal. 6:1, R.V.); by admonishing the disorderly; encouraging the fainthearted; supporting the weak; being longsuffering toward all (I Thess. 5:14, R.V.); by avoiding that by which a brother stumbles (Rom. 14:15, 21, R.V.); by following after peace, and wherewith one may edify others (Rom. 14:19); but never despairing (Luke 6:35); by being kind, tenderhearted, forgiving to one another, even as God in Christ forgave us (Eph. 4:32, R.V.); by giving of our means to meet another's need (II Cor. 8:24; I John 3:17); by kindly affection toward others (Rom. 12:10).

Love to those who do personal wrong is manifested by rebuke, first privately, then before one or two witnesses, then before the church (Matt. 18:15-17); to public offenders, rebuke in sight of all (I Tim. 5:20, R.V.).

Love for others is manifested by prayer for them—in no other way can we do more (Matt. 5:44, R.V.); for the brethren, by laying down our lives for them (John 15:13; I John 3:16, R.V.). (See also I Cor. 13:4-7.)

Love is indispensable to man; eloquence, gifts, knowledge, faith, sacrifice, martyrdom—all are of no value if love is lacking (I Cor. 13:1-3, R.V.); love is greater than faith and hope (I Cor. 13:13, R.V.); love never fails (I Cor. 13:8, R.V.).

Love to one another is the sum of God's commandment, the original and fundamental message of Christianity, Christ's new and all-inclusive commandment (John 13:34; I John 3:11, 23); it is the royal law (James 2:8), the bond that unites all the virtues together into a perfect whole (Col. 3:14, R.V.). Note also verses 12 and 13.

Love is the supreme and decisive test of our knowing God (I John 4:8), of our being born of God, and being children of God (I John 3:10; 4:7); of our having passed out of death into life (I John 3:14, R.V.); of our abiding in God and God in us (I John 4:12, 16); of love to God (I John 4:20); it is the one thing above all else which we are to seek to have. Paul, John, James, Peter and Jesus with one voice proclaim the supremacy of love.

Love covers a multitude of sins (I Peter 4:8); builds up (I Cor. 8:1, R.V.); knits together (Col. 2:2); and love to the brethren gives prevailing power to prayer (I John 3: 22, 23).

Faith works by love; love is the outcome of faith (Gal. 5:6; cf. I John 3:23). Love is greater than faith, but faith is the root of love, the root of which love is the fruit. To say "it is better to have love even without faith than it is to have faith without love," is much like saying it is better to have a crop of apple trees, than to have roots without apples. Rootless trees do not bear fruit, and faithless lives do not bring forth love.

Love is the fruit of the Spirit (Gal. 5:22; Rom. 5:5), and we will never attain to love by any mere effort of our own, for love is not a fruit that is native to the soil of the human heart. We should follow after love (I Cor. 14:1, R.V.; I Tim. 6:11), and we should urge one another to love (Heb. 10:24). God teaches us to love one another (I Thess. 4:9), and He imparts increasing love in answer to prayer (Phil. 1:9).

If you would learn to love, let Christ live His life in your heart; renounce self; renounce the flesh; crucify it; put it in the place of the curse, and let Christ live His life in you (Gal. 2:20).

THE HOLY SPIRIT—That the Holy Spirit is a divine Person is attested by Scripture (John 15:26; 16:7-14).

In Old Testament times He did not abide *in* man, but *with* man, coming upon whom He would. Christ, during His ministry, told the disciples that the Spirit could be had by asking (Luke 11:13), promising later that the Spirit would come to abide with them forever, in answer to His prayer to the Father (John 14:16, 17). This promise was fulfilled on the Day of Pentecost. After His resurrection, and in the upper room, He had breathed upon them saying, "Receive the Holy Spirit" (John 20:22, R.S.V.), and directed them to remain in Jerusalem until endued with the Spirit's power before commencing their ministry. On the day of Pentecost, they were all filled with the Holy Spirit (Acts 2:1-4), and it was upon that day that the kingdom was opened to the Jews (Acts 2:39), after which time the Spirit was bestowed on Jewish believers by the laying on of hands (Acts 8:17). When the kingdom was opened to the Gentiles (Acts 10), the Holy Spirit fell upon the listeners while Peter was still speaking (v. 44); and now, during this present age, the Spirit has dwelt on earth, indwelling every believer (I Cor. 6:19; Rom. 8:9-15), baptizing every believer (I Cor. 12:13; I John 2:20-27), so sealing him for God (Eph. 1:13).

There is also a "filling with the Spirit" (Eph. 5:18), which, often repeated, is the believer's privilege; but it should not be confused with the permanent indwelling of the Spirit.

The Lord Jesus was conceived by the Spirit (Matt. 1:18-20; Luke 1:35); the Holy Spirit was present at Jesus' baptism (Matt. 3:16; Mark 1:10; Luke 3:22; John 1:32, 33); was with Jesus at Satan's temptation (Matt. 4:1; Luke 4:1), and in His ministry (Luke 4:14); was the power of Jesus' resurrection (Rom. 8:11); and is His witness during the age of grace (John 15:26; 16:8, 14).

The Holy Spirit builds the Church, that structure of living stones, which grows through the salvation of souls through the Spirit's power (Eph. 2:18-22).

Scripture tells of certain sins that can be committed against the Spirit by the unsaved: blaspheming (Matt. 12:31), resisting (Acts 7:51), insulting (Heb. 6:29). Believers' sins against the Spirit are: grieving Him with evil (Eph. 4:30, 31); quenching of the Spirit by sinning (I Thess. 5:19).

Types or symbols of the Spirit are: oil (John 3:34); water (John 7:38, 39); wind (Acts 2:2); fire (Acts 2:3); the dove (Matt. 3:16); the seal (Eph. 1:13); an earnest (pledge or promise) (Eph. 1:14).

BOOK OF LIFE, LAMB'S BOOK OF LIFE, THE BOOKS THAT WERE OPENED—The book of life is the book of the living, and is a record, too, of their profession; from this book names may be blotted out (Rev. 3:5). Some names, those of Christian believers, will never be blotted out, but will remain there right through "from before the foundation of the world"; but others, those of the lost, are blotted out, and the gaping, empty spaces, where their names might have been, are shown to them at the judgment of the Great White Throne (Rev. 20:11-15), where "the books were opened." These are the books containing the records of their works, by which it will be shown that all are guilty before God; they will be sentenced according to the enormity of their offenses; it is written that "whosoever is not found written in the book of life was cast into the lake of fire."

The Lamb's book of life is a separate book; it is the record of the eternal purpose of God, and the names inscribed therein are written, through God's foreknowledge, "from before the foundation of the world" (Rev. 13:8; 21:27), and can never be blotted out. In other words, the book of life speaks of responsibility; the Lamb's book of life of pure grace. No names will ever be blotted out of the Lamb's book of life, for all written therein have eternal life, which is unforfeitable and everlasting.

THE MILLENNIUM OR KINGDOM AGE—Nowhere in Scripture is the word "millennium" found. But Revelation 20 speaks six times of a "thousand years," and "millennium" is the Latin equivalent meaning a "thousand years." This will be the time of a great age of righteousness upon the earth, when all nations will be subject to the lordship of Jesus Christ before time has run its course. Psalm 72:4-11, 17 says, "He shall judge the poor of the people, he shall save the children of the needy, and shall break in pieces the oppressor. They shall fear thee as long as the sun and the moon endure, throughout all generations. He shall come down like rain upon the mown grass; as showers that water the earth. In his days shall the righteous flourish; and abundance of peace so long as the moon endureth. He shall have dominion also from sea to sea, and from the river unto the ends of the earth. They that dwell in the wilderness shall bow before him; and his enemies shall lick the dust. The kings of Tarshish and of the isles shall bring presents; the kings of Sheba and Seba shall offer gifts. Yea, all kings shall fall down before him: all nations shall serve him . . . his name shall endure forever: his name shall be continued as long as the sun: and men shall be blessed in him: all nations shall call him blessed." Now, it has never been true in the past that all kings have made obeisance to Him and all nations have served Him, or that all nations have called Him blessed; but such a time of blessing must yet come for this poor world.

In Revelation 20 we learn that a time will come when Satan, the great enemy of God and man, will be bound for a thousand years, and will be unable to go out to deceive the nations until the thousand years are finished. The first resurrection, we are told, will take place at the beginning of that thousand years; the resurrected saints will live and reign with Christ for a thousand years. The rest of the dead will not be raised until the thousand years are finished; after the thousand years is the judgment of the Great White Throne. Certainly nothing answering to this thousand-year period has ever been known on this earth.

"And in the days of these kings shall the God of heaven set up a kingdom, which shall never be destroyed: and the kingdom shall not be left to other people, but it shall break in pieces and consume all these kingdoms, and it shall stand forever" (Dan. 2:44). This is the fifth great dominion that will bear rule over all the earth; it surely has not arrived up to the present time, and can only be the Lord Jesus Christ's kingdom during the millennial age. The same is true concerning similar predictions of Daniel 7:13, 14, 22, 27.

Characteristics of this time of blessing come before us in many other passages and can be noticed under seven distinct heads:

1. *The regeneration of Israel, who will become a blessing*

to all the earth. This is clearly predicted in Isaiah 60:1-22. Chapter 61 takes up the same wondrous story, as does Jeremiah 31; see also Zechariah 14:16-21.

2. *A warless world.* The Lord Jesus Christ tells us that wars and rumors of wars will characterize the entire present period (Matt. 24:6). (See Isa. 2:2-5; Micah 4:1-5.) Who would presume to say that swords have been beaten into plowshares, or that nations have laid down the sword and make war no more? Yet it is clearly predicted for this world before time will end.

3. *Poverty abolished.* These same Scriptures also tell us of a time when all men will enjoy temporal comfort when "they shall sit every man under his vine and under his fig tree; and none shall make them afraid" (Mic. 4:4). Zechariah gives the same testimony, and Isaiah (65:21-23) confirms it.

4. *Changed conditions of the lower creation.* When this time of blessing comes, even the lower creation will share in it. "The wolf and the lamb shall feed together, and the lion shall eat straw like the bullock; and dust shall be the serpent's meat. They shall not hurt nor destroy in all my holy mountain, saith the Lord" (Isa. 65:25). (See also Isa. 11:6-9.)

5. *Sickness will practically disappear from the earth.* "And the inhabitant shall not say, I am sick" (Isa. 33:24).

6. *Death will no longer be prevalent, but inflicted only judicially.* Notice carefully Isaiah 65:18-20. It is very evident from this Scripture that in the coming day of Jehovah's power those who enter into millennial blessings on the earth will, under ordinary circumstances, be granted the gift of long life, such as the patriarchs enjoyed before the Flood. In fact, it would seem that they would live right on through the entire period, unless there be some willful sin that will be dealt with immediately in judgment; under such circumstances we read that a sinner dying at the age of one hundred years

will be as the death of a child. This shows us that the kingdom age will not be like the eternal state in which sin can never again lift up its head and death will be absolutely unknown. It will still be possible for man to sin against divine light even if there be no adversary to tempt him; but such behavior will not be tolerated when righteousness begins and reigns, without immediate judicial dealing.

7. *Righteousness will be everywhere triumphant.* During the present time we are called upon to suffer for righteousness' sake. In the kingdom age "a king shall reign in righteousness, and princes shall rule in judgment" (Isa. 32:1). This will be the time when God's "judgments are in the earth, the inhabitants of the world will learn righteousness" (Isa. 26:9). "Then judgment shall dwell in the wilderness, and righteousness remain in the fruitful field. And the work of righteousness shall be peace; and the effect of righteousness quietness and assurance forever. And my people shall dwell in peaceable habitation, and in sure dwellings, and in quiet resting places" (Isa. 32:16-18). "For the earth shall be filled with the knowledge of the glory of the Lord, as the waters cover the sea" (Hab. 2:14). These few passages declare the same general truth that ere God closes up the history of this world He will give to man a demonstration of life on earth at its very best—no tempting devil, no poverty and distress, no wickedness and corruption prevailing, no wasting sickness and disease, death itself practically banished, and divine authority everywhere established; thus it is that God is going to bring to pass in His own time, in accordance with His prophetic Word, the thousand-year age of righteousness on this earth, before time ends and eternity begins.

KINGDOM OF GOD AND KINGDOM OF HEAVEN —While the kingdom of God and the kingdom of Heaven are not the same, yet in many respects there is a great similarity or parallelism. However, they may be separated from each other by several characteristics: (1) the kingdom of God covers the divine authority over the entire universe at any and all times, and is all-inclusive of those willing to be controlled by God's will, whether angels or Old Testament and New Testament saints (Luke 13:28, 29; Heb. 12:22, 23); whereas the kingdom of Heaven has as its ultimate purpose the setting up of the kingdom of God on earth (I Cor. 15: 24, 25).

(2) The Lord Jesus asserts that entrance into the kingdom of God is only through the new birth, by being born again (John 3:3, 5-7); the kingdom of Heaven covers the entire sphere of profession, true or false (it is Christendom) during the time of the King's absence, as in the parables of the kingdom of Heaven (Matt. 13, etc.). Because of the parallelism between the two, many parables of Matthew refer to the kingdom of Heaven, while in Mark and Luke to the kingdom of God. It is important, however, that the parables of the wheat, the tares and the net (Matt. 13:24-30, 36-43, 47-50) are not told of the kingdom of God; for in it are no tares, no bad fish. The parable of the leaven, however, is told of both kingdoms, for even the very truths of the kingdom are contaminated by "leaven" (teaching) of the Pharisees and others.

(3) The kingdom of God is spiritual, of the heart, as is seen from John 3; Romans 14:17; Luke 17:20; while the kingdom of Heaven is visible and will be the glorious, displayed kingdom of the Lord Jesus Christ, established on this earth (Luke 1:31-33).

(4) The kingdom of Heaven will be absorbed by the kingdom of God when Christ delivers up the kingdom to God the Father (I Cor. 15:24-28).

KEYS OF THE KINGDOM—"And I will give unto thee the keys of the kingdom of heaven; and whatsoever thou shalt bind on earth shall be bound in heaven; and whatsoever thou shalt loose on earth shall be loosed in heaven" (Matt. 16:19). Notice that in this verse the pronouns are singular: "thee" and "thou" cannot apply to the whole company of the apostles. If the others were included the pronouns would be "ye" and "you." Neither must this passage be confused with Matthew 18:18, which deals with Church discipline. Here Peter alone is in view; also, the keys are not to Heaven, but to the kingdom of Heaven.

The act of Christ in delivering the keys of the kingdom of Heaven into Peter's hands, with authority to bind or to loose, will become clear if we are careful to search for its meaning only in the Scriptures themselves. The Lord Jesus was about to leave the earth, to be absent for a long time. It was needful that the King, before His departure, should make it known who could enter the kingdom, and upon what conditions. The New Testament had not yet been written. He here selects Peter, His first convert, to speak for Him in this regard.

If Peter's movements are carefully traced after his Lord's departure, it will be found that it is he, and he alone, who opened the doors of the kingdom of Heaven. There were three of these keys received by Peter from the Lord Jesus' hands. The first was used on that great Day of Pentecost, when Peter was the spokesman, and when he opened the doors of the kingdom *to the people of Israel*. "The promise is unto you," said he, "and to your children, and to all that are afar off, even as many as the Lord our God shall call" (Acts 2:39; cf. Dan. 9:7). To be sure, the other disciples preached on that day, but Peter had to be present and approving. He was the chief spokesman.

Again, after the persecution that arose after the death of

Stephen, Philip went to Samaria, and preached to the Samaritans; but though many believed the Word, the Holy Spirit fell on none of them. "Now when the apostles that were at Jerusalem heard that Samaria had received the Word of God, they sent unto them Peter and John: who, when they were come down prayed for them, that they might receive the Holy Spirit: for as yet it was fallen on none of them: only they had been baptized into the name of the Lord Jesus. Then they laid their hands on them, and they received the Holy Spirit" (Acts 8:14-17, R.V.). This was Peter's second key. He had now opened the doors of the kingdom to the *Jews* and the *Samaritans*. (The Samaritans were, strictly speaking, neither Jews nor Gentiles, but a mixture of the two.)

The third and last key was used in Acts 10, to open these doors to the Gentile world. Cornelius, the Roman centurion, was commanded by an angel of God to send to Joppa for Peter; and Peter, by the vision of the great sheet, was shown that even the unclean Gentiles were no longer unclean. For God had cleansed them. Peter went to Cornelius' house and preached the gospel to those assembled there. Peter was not the apostle to the Gentiles; that was Paul's office, and Paul was converted in the preceding chapter. But Peter, the apostle to the circumcision, must be the first to take the gospel to the uncircumcision, for Peter had the keys. In each of these three instances, God showed, by the visible descent of the Holy Spirit upon the hearers, that what Peter was doing upon the earth was ratified in Heaven. Never again was there any use for the keys to the kingdom, for the doors were wide open, so that all who would might come. In the case of the Ephesians, who had received only John's baptism (Acts 19), Peter's presence was not needed, for he had already opened the door to *all* the Gentiles.

MYSTERIES OF THE KINGDOM—In Matthew 13 are seven parables, termed by the Lord Jesus Christ "mysteries of the kingdom of heaven" (v. 11). These seven parables, collectively, show forth the sphere on earth where Christ's authority is professedly owned, and His Word honored, even if only in an outward way; they depict the results of the presence of the Word in the world during the time of sowing the seed, the present age of grace (extending from the Lord's days on earth to the end of the age, the "harvest" of vv. 40-43). It is the word of the kingdom, and all who profess to receive it constitute the kingdom of the heavens in its present mystical form, being practically synonymous with "Christendom."

LEAVEN—Leaven is used in the New Testament as a symbol, and is *never* a symbol of anything good, but throughout is evil and false. The Lord Jesus warns against the "leaven of the Pharisees and Sadducees" (Matt. 16:6), and of Herod (Mark 8:15), which is evil doctrine (v. 12). This leaven of the Pharisees was hypocrisy in religion; of the Sadducees, unbelief in the resurrection (Matt. 22:23); of Herod, world politics mixed with religion (Matt. 22:15-21). Paul writes of "the leaven of malice and wickedness," and contrasts it with "the unleavened bread of sincerity and truth" (I Cor. 5:6-8). In Revelation 2:20 there is the woman Jezebel, typifying the false church, and insinuating the evil doctrines (leaven) with the truth of Scripture. Leaven is also always mentioned in the Old Testament in a manner and sense that is evil.

PARABLE OF THE MUSTARD SEED—"Another parable he put before them, saying, 'The kingdom of heaven is like a grain of mustard seed which a man took and sowed in his field; it is the smallest of all seeds, but when it has grown it is the greatest of shrubs and becomes a tree, so that the birds of the air come and make nests in its branches'" (Matt. 13:31, 32, R.S.V.).

Here we have the outward development of the kingdom of the heavens as it grows and expands, in an unnatural way, and becomes the roosting place of the birds of heaven. The almost universal comment on this mustard seed and its miraculous growth, as it is termed, is that it fully declares the expansion of the Church, and the birds of heaven are interpreted as meaning peoples and nations, who find shelter in the Church. Growing and still growing, the mustard seed reaches over the entire earth, its branches spread out wider and wider, and soon (so they tell us) the tree will have covered the earth as the waters cover the deep.

If the Lord had meant His Church by this mustard seed, which becomes a tree and a roosting place for birds, then this parable would be in flagrant contradiction with what He and the Holy Spirit teach elsewhere concerning the Church in the earth, the mission and the future of the Church, and the greatest clash of teaching would be the result.

For instance, in His prayer our Lord says concerning His own, those who are one as the Father and Son are one: "They are not of the world, as I am not of the world" (John 17:14). The Church, then, composed of all true believers, is not of the world as He is not of the world. The church is from above, as every believer has a life which is from above; but for a little while the church is *in* the world, and in a little while the Church will be above, where He is the glorified Head of His Body.

The mustard seed springing up in the field (remember, the field is the world, as our Lord tells us), rooting deeper and deeper in the earth, and expanding in this unnatural way affording room for birds, is the picture of something entirely different. It shows us a system which is rooted in the earth, and which aims at greatness in the world, expansion over the earth. The Lord never meant His Church to be rooted and grounded in the field, the world. He never called the Church to assume such proportions and become an abnormal growth in the earth. Whatever is spoken of Christ is spoken of the Church. Suffering and glory, after lowliness, followed by exaltation, is the way the Church goes; it is the way ordained for the Church. It is to be lowly, now suffering with Him, rejected and disowned by the world as He was, never to reign and rule now; but patiently waiting for Him for the moment when He is manifested, and *then* to share His throne and His glory. The calling and destiny of the Church are heavenly, and its mission is to reflect Him and testify to His grace, but never to control and to overspread the world. The epistles addressed to the Church make this sufficiently clear.

But if the mustard seed and its growth does not mean the *Church*, what does it mean? It means the kingdom of the heavens, and this is *professing Christendom*, which includes the whole sphere of Christian profession during this age, both saved and unsaved, Romanists and Protestants, all who are naming the name of Christ; therefore the Church is not the kingdom of the heavens, though the Church is in the kingdom of the heavens. At once the parable becomes illuminated with light; looked upon in this light, in full harmony with all the Lord teaches in this chapter, all is easily understood. The little mustard seed, which was not destined to be a tree but only a shrub, easily taken out of the ground where it had been planted, develops against its nature into a tree. That which came from Him, the Son of Man, the Sower, develops when committed into the hands of men, into an unnatural thing—one might say a monstrosity—for such a mustard *tree is*. This unnatural thing, this monstrosity, is professing Christendom as a system in the world, *professing*

79

Christ without possessing Him and His Spirit.

Attention is now called to the third message to the churches in Revelation 2, the one to Pergamum, typifying the age of the history of Christendom, beginning with Constantine the Great. The suffering and persecuted Church was made a state church. The mustard seed suddenly became the tree, and ever since the professing church has delighted in looking upon itself as a big expanding tree. But notice the perfect agreement of the third parable and the third church message.

The birds which roost in that tree would mean, if the parable applies to the Church, converted sinners; but the birds never represent clean persons, and it is unnecessary to go outside of the chapter to see this. The birds which fell upon the seed fallen by the wayside were instruments of Satan; birds of heaven, or fowls, never mean anything good in Scripture. Abraham stood in the midst of the pieces of the sacrifices and drove away the fowls which were ready to fall upon them (Gen. 15); the fowls there represented nothing good. Birds in this parable mean unsaved, unconverted people and nations, who flock for selfish motives to the tree, the outward form of Christendom, and find shelter there, but they defile the tree.

At last the tree will be full grown. Of the full-grown tree it is said, "Babylon the great . . . has become the habitation [roosting place] of demons, and a hold of every unclean spirit, and a hold of every *unclean and hateful bird*" (Rev. 18:2).

But do not forget that there is a tree which is to grow up and spread its branches, taking sap out of the root, over the whole earth. This tree is Israel—the good olive tree with its indestructible root. Some of the branches are now broken off and lie upon the ground. Romans 11 assures us, however, that God is able to graft them in again. Yet, before this olive tree with its Holy Root, this olive tree with its long-promised future, the covenant made with an oath, stands high-minded, boasting Christendom, boasting itself against the branches, and claiming to be the tree to overspread the earth and thus attending to Israel's calling. Alas! the warning is cast into the winds, "If God spared not the natural branches, take heed lest he spare not thee." What a fall it will be when at last that tree, the monstrous tree, falls and is destroyed forever, root and all!

PARABLE OF THE LEAVEN—Another parable spake He unto them: "The kingdom of heaven is like unto leaven, which a woman took, and hid in three measures of meal, till the whole was leavened" (Matt. 13:33).

This fourth parable has been a battleground for commentators. There is no need of confusion, if the authority of the Scriptures is recognized and allowed to interpret the parable. The popular conception that the leaven is the gospel of Christ, and that this gospel is to pervade and permeate the world until the world is saved, is without scriptural basis. Not only does such an interpretation place our Lord in the position of contradicting all His other parables by the use of this one, but it also destroys the whole Bible as the source of authority in the matter of its own understanding and interpretation. Now, comparing spiritual things with spiritual, it is found that leaven is never once used in the Word of God except as a type of corruption. In connection with the first Passover, Israel was commanded to put away leaven out of their houses (Exod. 12:15). In Leviticus 2:11, the law provided that no meal offering should be made with leaven. In Leviticus 6:17, in the law of the meal offering, it is written, "It shall not be baken with leaven. . . . It is most holy." The two wave-loaves of the Pentecostal offering (Lev. 23:17) were baked with leaven, because they typified the Church of

81

God, and signified that we are accepted in the Beloved despite our indwelling evil nature; for He was made sin for us.

In His personal ministry our Lord often used leaven as a type of evil. At one time His disciples forgot to take a supply of bread with them, and Jesus said to them, "Take heed and beware of the leaven of the Pharisees and Sadducees. And they reasoned among themselves, saying, It is because we took no bread." But Jesus explained His words, and "then understood they how that he bade them not to beware of the leaven of bread, but of the teachings of the Pharisees and Sadducees" (Matt. 16:5-12). In Luke 12:1 the Lord Jesus said to His disciples, "Beware of the leaven of the Pharisees, which is hypocrisy"; and in Mark 8:15 He also warned them against the leaven of Herod, evidently meaning lust for worldly power.

Leaven, then, is a figure of corruption. Now, who is the woman hiding the leaven in the meal? It is significant that this is the only mention of a woman in the seven parables of the chapter. She is easily recognized as the false professing church, corrupting by false doctrine and sinful conduct, the food of the children, which is the Word of God. Hiding the leaven in the meal, she leaves it there, and the corrupting process continues until the true food is all gone, being utterly lost in the repulsive and poisonous mass—the whole lump leavened.

It was against this awful danger that Paul later warned the Galatian churches, which were receiving the Judaizing teachers. With the Lord's parable of the leaven in mind he wrote: "Ye were running well; who did hinder you, that ye should not obey the truth? This persuasion came not of him that calleth you. A little leaven leaveneth the whole lump. I have confidence in you through the Lord, that ye will be none otherwise minded; but he that troubleth you shall bear his judgment, whoever he be" (see Gal. 5:7-10).

And again when the Corinthian church was indulging in sinful practices, the apostle wrote: "It is actually reported that there is fornication among you, and such fornication that is not even among the Gentiles, that one of you has his father's wife. And ye are puffed up, and did not rather mourn, that he that did this deed might be taken away from among you. . . . Your glorying is not good. Know ye not that a little leaven leaveneth the whole lump? Purge out the old leaven, that ye may be a new lump, even as ye are unleavened. For our Passover also hath been sacrificed, even Christ: wherefore let us keep the feast, not with old leaven of malice and wickedness, but with the unleavened bread of sincerity and truth" (I Cor. 5:1-8, R.V.). And so it is seen that in Scripture language leaven never means anything good, and it *always* stands for evil and corruption. The ones to whom our Lord spoke were Jews, and they certainly understood what was meant by leaven. No Jew would ever dream that leaven used in illustrating some power or process, could stand for something good—leaven to the Jews *always* meant evil.

And now the question of the three measures of meal and what they represent: the accepted, but faulty teaching is that the Lord means corrupted humanity by it. However, this is as impossible as it is for leaven to be something good. Where does the meal come from? Surely any child can answer that— the meal comes from the *wheat*. Tares, the type for evil, never yield fine, wholesome meal; meal is the product of the good seed only. Good, nutritious and pure as it is, it can never represent the unregenerated mass of humanity. But there is still greater evidence: three measures of meal *stand for Christ in type*, the corn of wheat and the bread of life; when Abraham comforted the Lord (Gen. 18) it was by three measures of meal and a calf, typical of Christ, His Person and His work. He is good, pure, holy, undefiled, as well as that which He has given, His Word. It is therefore folly to twist Scripture language around and make the three measures of meal mean corruption, when meal always denotes purity.

PARABLE OF THE TREASURE—"The kingdom of heaven is like unto a treasure hidden in the field; which a man found, and hid; and in his joy he goeth and selleth all that he hath, and buyeth that field" (Matt. 13:44, R.V.). We shall never have the kingdom manifested here until the King comes back, and He is coming back; just as truly as He went away, He will return. In the first verse of this chapter this is carefully indicated. There He is seen departing from Israel, and turning to the Gentiles; "He went out of the house and sat by the seaside," the "house" which He left being typical of Israel, and the "sea" that He came to, typical of the Gentiles. But He has not forgotten Israel. In verse 36 it is written, "Then he left the multitudes, and went into the house"; He is ever true and faithful, and Israel is still beloved for the fathers' sake; in this parable He has His kinsmen in mind.

The treasure is Israel, now hidden in the field, which is the world, as our Lord has told us. The man, who in his joy goes and sells all and buys the field, is the Lord Jesus Christ Himself. It was on the cross of Calvary that He paid the price; He sold all He had, and by right of purchase, as well as by right of creation, the world (the field) is His. "The earth is the Lord's, and the fullness thereof; the world, and they that dwell therein" (Ps. 24:1). And Israel is His treasure, now hidden, but one day to be brought forth in glory. "Israel shall blossom and bud and fill the face of the world with fruit" (Isa. 27:6). In that day they shall remember and obey His word, as He said, "If ye will obey my voice indeed, and keep my covenant, then ye shall be a peculiar treasure to me above all people: for all the earth is mine. And ye shall be unto me a kingdom of priests, and an holy nation" (Exod. 19:5, 6; Ps. 135:4).

PARABLE OF THE PEARL—"Again, the kingdom of heaven is like unto a man that is a merchant, seeking goodly pearls: who, when he had found one pearl of great price, went and sold all that he had, and bought it" (Matt. 13:45, 46). The man here is also none other than the blessed Lord Jesus Christ. He came seeking goodly pearls, to seek and to save that which was lost. Pearls are found at the bottom of the sea, and the sea again represents the Gentile world. He has visited the Gentiles to take out of them a people for His name. The pearl of great price is the true Church, and its value may speak to us of the glory of His inheritance in the saints (Eph. 1:18). The pearl is one for it typifies the one body. The great price was His own precious blood, paid on the cross: "Ye are bought with a price." In order to pay that price He yielded all that He had; He hath redeemed us, and now we are His. (See I Peter 1:18, 19.)

PARABLE OF THE DRAGNET—"Again, the kingdom of heaven is like a net which was thrown into the sea and gathered fish of every kind; when it was full, men drew it ashore and sat down and sorted the good into vessels but threw away the bad. So will it be at the close of the age. The angels will come out and separate the evil from the righteous, and throw them into the furnace of fire; there men will weep and gnash their teeth" (Matt. 13:47-50, R.S.V.).

This is not the "gospel net," as it is often called. After the one pearl is taken up, the end of the age begins. This parable falls into the completion of the age. The dragnet is let into the sea, which, as we have seen before, represents the nations, Gentiles. The parable refers to the preaching of the "everlasting gospel" as it will take place during the Great Tribulation (Rev. 14:6, 7). The separating of the good and bad is done by the angels. All this cannot refer to the present time nor to the Church, but to the time when the kingdom is about to be set up. Then angels will be used, as is so clearly seen in the Book of the Revelation. The wicked will be cast into the furnace of fire, and the righteous will remain in the earth for the millennial kingdom. It is the same "end of the age" described in Matthew 24.

SERMON ON THE MOUNT—The Sermon on the Mount (Matt. 5-7), is not the way of salvation for the sinner, nor the rule of life for the Christian. When the Lord Jesus preached it, He had not yet established His Church. The Sermon on the Mount is law, and the Christian is not under law but under grace. If the Sermon on the Mount then be neither the way of life for the sinner, nor the rule of life for the believer, but is law, then it becomes evident that it is the code of laws for the kingdom of Heaven, which kingdom, though for the time being rejected, will one day be set up on this earth. Its capital will be Jerusalem, and the law shall go forth from Zion. In that day "Jehovah shall be King over all the earth; in that day shall Jehovah be one and his name one" (see Zech. 14:9; Ps. 2:6; Jer. 23:5).

In the Sermon on the Mount there is this King, Jehovah-Jesus, formally offering the kingdom to Israel, in His own Person. The offer is made in Galilee, for it had already been offered by John the Baptist in Judea and rejected. The King, in this great discourse, plainly sets forth the nature of the proposed kingdom, and the laws by which He will govern the earth when He re-establishes and occupies the throne of David, upon His return to this earth.

However, there is value in the Sermon on the Mount to the Church, for it is part of Scripture, and all Scripture is valuable. Believers, who are members of His Church, are destined to reign over the kingdom, and therefore should be deeply interested in the laws of the kingdom. In addition, many eternal principles are expressed in the Sermon, which are always operative; it is true even now that the poor in spirit are "blessed"; that those who mourn, in the fellowship of His sufferings, shall be comforted; true that the merciful shall obtain mercy, and that the pure in heart do see God.

While Luke gives a sermon somewhat similar, it is not the same, and the Sermon on the Mount appears only in Matthew, where it is fitting that the laws of the kingdom should be recorded in the gospel of the kingdom.

THE BEATITUDES—The beatitudes of Matthew 5 are the beginning of the so-called Sermon on the Mount, and they too are found only in the Gospel of Matthew. The King's proclamation took place in the presence of great multitudes from Galilee and the Decapolis, Jerusalem, and Judea, and from beyond the Jordan (4:25), though it was addressed directly to His own disciples, heirs of the kingdom, whom He called apart unto Himself, and apart from the crowd (5:1). He began by describing in seven beatitudes the heirs to the kingdom, as to their character. Mark this, He is describing persons, not as they ought to be, nor as they ought to try to be, *but as they are.* They are His workmanship; by the grace of God they are what they are. They have not become what they are by their own striving, but by His favor and power; it is God working in them, both to will and to do of His own good pleasure (Phil. 2:13).

1. "Blessed are the poor in spirit, for theirs is the kingdom of heaven." They discovered their utter poverty, and taking the place of paupers before God, they suddenly became rich. Having nothing, and deserving nothing in themselves, all things became theirs. All this was because of the grace of the

Lord Jesus Christ, who, though He was rich, yet for their sakes became poor, that they, through His poverty, might be rich (II Cor. 8:9).

2. "Blessed are they that mourn, for they shall be comforted." Having come to know the Lord Jesus, they became, like Him, men of sorrows and acquainted with grief. This is their high privilege, not only to believe on Him, but also to suffer with Him; this is fellowship with His sufferings; it is a just sympathy with Him, seeing things as He sees them, and feeling with Him as He yearns over this lost world. They shall be comforted when He is comforted. When He sees the travail of His soul and is satisfied, then shall they, too, be satisfied, awakening with His likeness.

3. "Blessed are the meek, for they shall inherit the earth." The Spirit of the Master is upon them, and He is meek and lowly in heart. Meekness is never a human product; it is ever the fruit of the Spirit. It speaks of surrender to God, knowing His way is best. They shall inherit the earth, for it belongs to Christ, and Christ belongs to them, and they to Him. Children of God are they, and heirs jointly with Christ.

4. "Blessed are they that hunger and thirst after righteousness, for they shall be filled." No unsaved sinner ever hungered or thirsted after righteousness. He may desire mercy, but he knows if righteousness were meted out to him it would mean death. It is natural that the sinner under sentence of death should desire anything but righteousness. But it is different with the heir to the kingdom; he has met the claims of the law, having died unto it in the person of his Substitute, and now his whole soul yearns within him for righteousness. The will of God, once terrible to him, has become his meat and drink. And he shall be filled! Blessed be God for that promise! He shall be filled and lack nothing, having righteousness, and nothing but righteousness within him.

Sin all gone, and he filled with righteousness. Not yet is this true for Christians; though we are in our standing before Him free from sin, yet the fight with the flesh is not over. But in that day we shall be filled with unmixed righteousness.

5. "Blessed are the merciful, for they shall obtain mercy." This is the first beatitude of the last section, for like all the sevens in Matthew, this seven is divided into a four and a three. The first four, this being the earth number, describe the earthly condition of the heirs while waiting for the kingdom to appear. The final three, this being the heavenly number, speak of the heirs exercising their official functions in the kingdom. First, then, they are merciful, for they have become partakers of the divine nature. And the mercy that they themselves received is not earned or attained by their own mercy toward others; rather, it is obtained as a gift.

6. "Blessed are the pure in heart, for they shall see God." The purity here is not mere cleanness of heart, but rather singleness of heart. The heart is fixed; it is fully occupied with God. They shall see God. Their communion with Him shall be uninterrupted, for they have free access by His grace.

7. "Blessed are the peacemakers, for they shall be called the sons of God." This is ever the highest, holiest work of the heirs of the kingdom. It is their joyous privilege to make peace between God and men. Christ has made peace through His cross, and God was in Christ reconciling the world unto Himself; but He has committed unto His disciples the ministry of reconciliation. And sonship can manifest itself in no surer way than this: God's sons holding forth the Word of Life that men may have peace with God. And where there is peace between man and God, there will always be peace between man and man.

This, then, is the seven-runged ladder by which the poor beggar mounts upward: "destitute, sorrowing, meek, hungry, he is forgiven, a trusted official, a son. Grace stands at the foot of the ladder, mercy in the middle, peace at the head; so the benediction of the beloved disciple sums up these beatitudes: 'grace, mercy, and peace from God the Father, and from the Lord Jesus Christ, the Son of the Father, in truth and love be with you.'"

These seven beatitudes are followed by two others, showing the real blessedness of their position in the world. If they are true heirs of the kingdom, the world will hate them and persecute them. This is a cause for rejoicing for them, for great is their reward in Heaven. The heirs of the kingdom are the salt of the earth, to arrest the process of corruption; the salt must be genuine or it is worthless. They are the light of the world, to light up the way to peace and safety, and the light must be allowed to shine, for the glory of the heavenly Father.

PROGRESS IN FELLOWSHIP—Progressive intimacy as depicted in the Gospel of John is: *Servants*: "Ye call me Master and Lord, and ye say well; for so I am" (John 13:13); *friends*: "Henceforth I call you not servants; for the servant knoweth not what his Lord doeth: but I have called you friends; for all things that I have heard of my Father I have made known unto you" (John 15:15); *brethren*: "Jesus said unto her, Touch me not; for I have not yet ascended to my Father: but go to my brethren and say unto them, I ascend unto my Father, and your Father; and to my God, and your God" (John 20:17).

SEPARATION—"Be ye separate" (II Cor. 6:17), an exhortation from Paul to all believers. In verse 14 Paul instructs believers not to be "unequally yoked" with unbelievers, which means as in marriage; membership in lodges, clubs, etc., part Christian and part non-Christian; partnerships in business with unbelievers; or any yoking together of believers with unbelievers for a common purpose. This can apply even to membership in some churches, many of which have become hopelessly alienated from God and His truth in their testimony.

Then there is separation from the world, meaning its system, in its evils, sins, lusts, pleasures, and the separation from false teaching (II John 9-11).

That separation is not meant to be from *contact* with evil in the world or the Church, but from participation in it, and acceptance of it as shown from I Corinthians 5:9-11, R.S.V. Paul says, "I wrote to you in my letter not to associate with immoral men; not at all meaning the immoral of this world, or the greedy and robbers, or idolaters, since then you would need to go out of the world. But rather I wrote to you not to associate with any one who bears the name of brother if he is guilty of immorality . . . not even to eat with such a one." Christ was "holy, harmless, undefiled, separated from sinners" (Heb. 7:26), yet in constant contact with them in the interest of their salvation, never to be understood by this world's hypocrites (Luke 7:34-39). Acceptance of the evils of this world-system is the loss of unbroken communion and fellowship with God, and service, all three of which separation holds intact (II Cor. 6:17, 18).

FOREKNOWLEDGE, ELECTION AND PREDESTINATION—In the divine sequence it is foreknowledge, election, predestination. Peter shows (I Peter 1:2) that election is according to God's foreknowledge, while predestination is the fulfilling of the election. It is perfectly clear in Scripture that God by His foreknowledge has predestinated all believers in the Lord Jesus Christ "to be conformed to the image of his Son" (Rom. 8:29), and all who believe were chosen in Christ "before the foundation of the world" (Eph. 1:4)

91

and their names written in the Lamb's Book of Life; so it will be seen that predestination is *never* to Heaven, nor yet to Hell, but always to special privilege in and with Christ. That salvation is not affected in any way by foreknowledge, election, or predestination is sure, for God says (John 3:16) that *whosoever* believes has eternal life, which is by grace through faith, and by man's free will. It has been said that the "whosoever wills" are the elect, the "whosoever won'ts" the nonelect.

ABIDING IN CHRIST—To bear fruit it is necessary for the branch to abide in the vine, and so for the believer to abide in Christ and Christ in the believer (John 15:4). To abide in Him, therefore, one's life must be as an open book to Him: no sins unjudged, and a daily walk where He can participate at all times. At the same time, one should take all cares and anxieties to Him for Him to bear, and allow nothing in life that could come between.

ADOPTION—"That we might receive the adoption of sons" (Gal. 4:4, 5). The Greek word for "adoption" is *huiothesia*, which means "placing as a son." It does not have the meaning that attaches to our English word "adoption" in modern usage. In ancient times a boy was not called a son until he came of age; then he was proclaimed as his father's son and heir, in a ceremony called *huiothesia*. God does not adopt those who are not His children already; adoption is related to position rather than to kinship. When a man is born again he becomes by that birth a child of God, and then God places him in the position of full sonship in His family. The Holy Spirit indwelling the believer assures him of this new position as a present experience. The full manifestation of this wonderful position, however, awaits the second coming of our Lord when the believer will receive his transfigured body. This fact is stated in Romans 8:23 where it says we wait "for the adoption, to wit, the redemption of our body."

CHRISTIAN CHARACTER—In Galatians 5: 22, 23 are enumerated nine graces called the "fruit of the Spirit." The embodying of these graces in the believer constitutes Christian character. The graces may be divided in their relationships as follows: love, joy and peace, the personal characteristics as related to the believer himself; longsuffering, gentleness, goodness, the believer's characteristics as manifested toward others; faith, meekness, temperance, the believer's characteristics as manifested toward God. Chapter 15 of John's Gospel contains the great discourse of our Lord upon fruit-bearing; in Galatians 5, the fruits are named. When possessed by the believer they are the effect of yielding, rather than of working.

WALKING IN THE LIGHT—To "walk in the light" (I John 1:7). God is "in the light," perfectly revealed in Christ. He wants man to walk "in the light"—not *according* to the light, but *in* the light. It is *where* one walks, not *how* one walks. It is in the presence of God, which the natural man does not want. But when convicted of sin and born again by the Holy Spirit, a person cannot stay away from that light, but makes his way into the very presence of One he once dreaded. How to continue to walk in the light is explained in I John 1:8-10: the realization of sin in self is recognized by the believer; upon confession of sins committed, he is at once forgiven and cleansed of all unrighteousness (v. 9). So, *as a sinner* the believer comes to Christ on the ground of this verse, and is cleansed; but *as a believer* confessing the failures of his life, he comes confessing his sin and He is "faithful and just to forgive"; judicial cleansing by the blood

93

of Christ, confession of sins for practical cleansing. Fellowship is disrupted by sin, but confession restores the fellowship.

REWARDS AND SALVATION—Salvation and rewards are carefully distinguished in Scripture. Salvation is a free gift of God to the lost (John 4:10; Rom. 6:23; Eph. 2:8, 9), while rewards are to the saved for faithful and meritorious service (Matt. 10:42; Luke 19:17; I Cor. 9:24, 25; Rev. 22:12). Salvation becomes both a present and an everlasting possession (John 3:36; 5:24; 6:47), while rewards are future and await the judgment seat of Christ at His second coming (I Cor. 3:11-15; II Cor. 5:10; Rom. 14:10).

Scripture enumerates five crowns offered as rewards: (1) The crown of rejoicing, for faithful service (I Thess. 2:19, 20; Phil. 4:1); (2) the crown of righteousness, for faithful testimony (II Tim. 4:8); (3) the crown of life, for faithfulness under trial (James 1:12; Rev. 2:10); (4) the crown of glory, for faithfulness in suffering (I Peter 5:4; Heb. 2:9); (5) the crown incorruptible, for faithfulness in exercising self-control in the race for Christ's approval (I Cor. 9:24-27).

STANDING AND STATE OF BELIEVER—The believer's *standing* (I Cor. 1:2-9) is his position in Christ, in the family of God. The believer's *state* (I Cor. 1:10-13) is his condition in that family, and it is dependent on, and varying with, his daily walk. The moment a sinner is born again he enters into a position in grace in the family of God, unchangeable for eternity; a standing that is the same for the weakest believer as for the greatest saint. He is a child of God and accepted in the Beloved (John 1:12, 13; Rom. 8:1, 15-17; I Cor. 12:12, 13; Gal. 3:26; Eph. 1:3-14; I Peter 2:9).

His state, on the other hand, may be far below his standing, his daily walk not fully in the Spirit. He is already a saint, and is called upon to walk as becometh a saint. The purpose of the indwelling Spirit is to bring his state up to his exalted standing, which He does through the application of the Word (John 17:17; Eph. 5:26); by chastening (I Cor. 11:32; Heb. 12:10); His own ministry (Eph. 4:11, 12); the ultimate consummation and complete change will be at the second coming of the Lord Jesus Christ (I John 3:2).

ADVOCACY—In John 13:10, the underlying imagery is of an Oriental returning from the public baths to his house. His feet would contract defilement and require cleansing but not his body. So the believer is cleansed as before the law from all sins "once for all" (Heb. 10:1-12); but he needs ever to bring his daily sins to the Father in confession, that he may abide in unbroken fellowship with the Father and with the Son (I John 1:1-10). The blood of Christ answers forever to all the law could say as to the believer's *guilt*, but he needs constant cleansing from the *defilement* of sin; see Ephesians 5:25, 27; I John 5:6. Typically, the order of approach to the presence of God was, first, the brazen altar of sacrifice, and then the laver of cleansing (Exod. 40:6, 7). Christ cannot have communion with a defiled saint, but He can and will cleanse him. Advocacy, therefore, is that work of Jesus Christ for sinning saints which He carries on with the Father, whereby because of the eternal efficacy of His own sacrifice, He restores them to fellowship (cf. Ps. 23:3).

ETERNAL LIFE—Without beginning and without ending, that is the sense of "eternal life," the life of God manifested in His Son and made an integral part of every human being born of the Holy Spirit (John 3:3-16). This life becomes an immediate and everlasting possession of the believer at the moment of belief (John 6:47), and does not wait on death for its beginning. The consummation for the believer will be at the resurrection, when the earthly body is changed to the eternal body, conforming to Christ's body.

FUTURE DESTINY OF BELIEVERS—(1) He who does God's will lives forever; the world and all it contains passes, but he continues (I John 2:17).

(2) He who believes on Jesus Christ, and keeps His Word shall never die (John 11:25, 26; 8:51); believers in Christ fall asleep, they do not die (cf. Acts 7:60); until Christ comes, believers who have departed this life are said to "sleep." (Note that sleep is not necessarily a state of unconsciousness, but oftentimes of the highest consciousness and mental activity; sleep is, however, usually a condition in which one is largely shut out to intercourse with the outside world, and shut up to God and His angels, or to the devil and his angels.)

(3) When the believer gets out of the flesh (the body) he departs to be with Christ; when he is absent from the body he is at home with the Lord (Phil. 1:23, 24; II Cor. 5:6-8); the Bible gives little information on this; it does say that this state "is very far better" than our present state (Phil. 1:23). This leaves no room for purgatorial tortures, nor for a state of unconsciousness; it is evidently a state of conscious bliss, but not the highest state the believer shall attain (II Cor. 5:1-4, 8).

(4) When Christ comes, the bodies of those who sleep in Christ shall be raised from the dead; not precisely the same bodies, however, even as the grain that grows is not precisely the same as the grain sown; the sown grain disintegrates and many of its constituent elements go, no one can say whither; but the formative principle takes to itself many new elements, no one can say whence; and so in the resurrection (I Thess. 4:16; I Cor. 15:12, 13, 20-23, 35-38).

(5) At the resurrection we shall be given, in place of the "earthly house of our tabernacle" (our present physical frame), "a building from God, a house not made with hands, eternal in the heavens" (the resurrection body). Mortality shall be swallowed up of life (II Cor. 5:1, 2, 4).

(6) At His coming our Saviour "shall fashion anew the body of our humiliation, that it may be conformed to the body of his glory" (Phil. 3:20, 21).

(7) At the resurrection of those who sleep in Jesus, believers who have remained alive until that time and those who are raised shall be caught up together to meet the Lord in the air (I Thess. 4:17); after that we shall ever be with the Lord (John 14:3; I Thess. 4:17; John 12:26). We shall be in a prepared place, a place where Jesus has gone for the express purpose of preparing it for us; we shall be a prepared people in a prepared place. This place that Jesus is preparing He speaks of as "abodes" or "abiding places" (translated "mansions" in A.V. See John 14:2). We shall be in a city which has foundations, whose builder and maker is God; a better country than this, a heavenly country; a city prepared of God for us (Heb. 11:10, 16). It will be an abiding city (Heb. 13:14), and we will not go to some building to worship, for the Lord God Almighty, and the Lamb are the temple thereof (Rev. 21:22). That city has no need of the sun, nor of the moon to shine upon it, for the glory of God lights it, and the Lamb Himself is the lamp thereof (Rev. 21:23). Paul got a hint of the dazzling brilliance of that light on the Damascus road. Our resurrection eyes will be able to endure and enjoy the glory that blinded him; the gates shall never be shut and there will be no night; perfect security and no darkness (Rev. 21:25); nothing unclean, nothing abominable, nothing false, untrue or unreal will be there; no saloons, no filth, no shams (Rev. 21:27). There shall be a river of water of life, bright

as crystal, flowing out of the throne of God and of the Lamb, in the midst of the street thereof; and on both sides of the river shall be the tree of life, bearing twelve fruits, yielding its fruit every month, and the leaves of the tree for the healing of the nations (Rev. 22:1, 2).

(8) We shall be like Him (I John 3:2), and we shall, with Him, be manifested in glory; not only beholding His glory, but reflecting it in ourselves (Col. 3:4), and the glory that God has given to Jesus shall be ours (John 17:22); we shall be sharers of God's own glory and kingdom; we shall be heirs of God and joint heirs with Jesus Christ, glorified together with Him (I Thess. 2:12; Rom. 8:17).

(9) We receive salvation through faith, but rewards will be given us according to our own works (Luke 19:12, 13, 15-19), and will vary in proportion to fidelity in service (cf Matt. 6:20; I Cor. 3:11-15). Among the rewards is the crown of life, being for those who endure temptation (trial), promised by the Lord to them that love Him (James 1:12); the crown of righteousness, for all those who "love his appearing" (II Tim. 4:8); the crown of glory for those undershepherds who have properly attended the flock of God during the absence of the Chief Shepherd (I Peter 5:1-4).

(10) God has promised, Christ has appointed, and it is the Father's good pleasure to give a kingdom to them that love God, and continue with Christ in His trials (James 2:5; Luke 22:28, 29; 12:32); in this kingdom we shall reign with Christ as priests of God and Christ (Rev. 20:6), a kingdom that was prepared for us from the foundation of the world (Matt. 25:34).

(11) To him that overcometh (carries off the victory) Christ will give to eat of the tree of life, which is in the Paradise of God (Rev. 2:7); he shall not be hurt of the second death (Rev. 2:11); Christ will give him of the hidden man-

na, a white stone, with a new name thereon, which no one knows but him who secures it (Rev. 2:17); also authority over the nations, and he shall rule them with a rod of iron (Rev. 2:26, 27); he shall be arrayed in white garments, and his name will be in the book of life, and Christ will acknowledge him before the Father and His angels (Rev. 3:4, 5); he will be made a pillar in God's temple, and upon him Christ will write the name of God, of the city of God, and His own new name (Rev. 3:12); he will sit down with Christ in His own throne (Rev. 3:21).

(12) God shall wipe away all tears from the eyes of His people; death shall be no more, and neither shall there be any mourning, crying or pain any more (Rev. 21:3, 4).

(13) We shall see no longer as in a mirror, in a riddle, but face to face; we shall no longer know only partly, but shall know God and all things perfectly, as He already knows us (I Cor. 13:12), and we shall be unreprovable in the day of the Lord Jesus Christ; He will so perfect us that there will be absolutely nothing in us that even He can be displeased with (I Cor. 1:8). So, we who are guarded by God's power, through faith, unto a salvation ready to be revealed in the last time, shall receive an inheritance, incorruptible and undefiled, that fadeth not away, reserved in Heaven for us.

ETERNAL SECURITY OF THE BELIEVER—The eternal security of the believer is this: once a sinner has been regenerated by the Word and Spirit of God, once he has received a new life and a new nature, and has been justified from every charge, it is absolutely impossible for him ever to be lost. The statement that the believer in the Lord Jesus Christ is eternally secure is based upon a number of lines of Scripture testimony. First, upon the perfection of Christ's one offering upon the cross; the Epistle to the Hebrews is a contrasting of the many sacrifices under law with the one sacrifice of our Lord Jesus Christ. The sacrifices under law never could take away sin; but in Hebrews 10 we are told that when the Lord Jesus Christ came into the world, and offered Himself without spot to God, the effect of His sacrifice was eternal. Verse 14 makes this clear: "For by one offering he hath perfected forever them that are sanctified." Perfected for as long as we are faithful? Not so—perfected *forever*. Why? because the sacrifice is efficacious.

To admit the possibility of a man's losing his salvation once he has been justified by faith, is a practical denial of the finished work of our Lord Jesus Christ. We are saved ternally because the sacrifice of Christ abides. The only round on which God could forgive sin is that Jesus settled for all on the cross, and when I trust Him, all that He has done goes down to my account.

Second, upon the perseverance and omnipotent power of the Holy Spirit of God. "Being confident of this very thing, that he which hath begun a good work in you will perform it until the day of Jesus Christ" (Phil. 1:6). The Holy Spirit began the good work in you, if you are a believer in the Lord Jesus. He convicted you of sin, led you to trust in Christ, gave you the witness through the Word that you were saved. Having thus taken you up in grace, the Holy Spirit has a definite purpose in view. He is going to eventually conform you fully to the image of the Lord Jesus Christ, and He never begins a work that He doesn't intend to finish. If He broke down your opposition to God when you were a sinner, surely He has power to subdue your will as a believer, and carry to completion the work He began.

Third, upon the fact of the new creation. In II Corinthians 5:17 (R.S.V.), we read, "Therefore, if anyone is in Christ, he is a new creation; the old has passed away, behold, the new has come." Once we were utterly lost, but we did not get into this place of spiritual death by any act of our own, but because we were born into the world members of the old creation of which Adam the first was head, and every child of Adam's race comes into the world lost and under sentence of death. In verse 14 it says "that if one died for all, then all were dead." As a result of Adam's failure, the old creation fell down in death, and every person born into the world since, was born down there; no one has been born up where Adam the first started, except our Lord Jesus Christ, and His birth was a supernatural one.

Therefore, as members of the old creation we were all dead, all lost; but our Lord Jesus Christ came into the world, the living Word, and He stood on this plane of sinlessness. Adam was created sinless but fell; Jesus, the sinless One, came, but He saw men down there in death, and at the cross He went down into death to where man was, and came up in grace from death. But not alone, for God has quickened us together with Christ, so that all who believe in Him are brought up from that place in death; as at one time we were made partakers of Adam's race, so now we are made partakers of a new creation. "He hath raised us up together, and made us to sit together in heavenly places with Christ Jesus" (Eph. 2:6), and because we belong to this new creation we can never be lost. You were lost because the head of the old creation failed, and you went down with him. You can never be lost unless the Head of the new creation fails, and if He does, you will go down with Him. But, thank God, He remains on the throne where God Himself has put Him, in token of the perfect satisfaction in the work He accomplished.

Fourth, upon the fact that the believer is the present possessor of eternal life. Believing on Him I have eternal life, but I have it in a dying body. I am now waiting for the redemption of the body; when the Lord Jesus comes the second time He will change this body of my humiliation and make it like unto the body of His glory. Then I shall have received eternal life in all its fullness, spirit, soul and body conformed to Christ. In that sense I am hoping for eternal life. But over, and over, and over again, Scripture rings out the fact that every believer is at the present time in possession of eternal life (John 3:14, 15). Adam's life was forfeitable; he lost his life because of sin. Eternal life is nonforfeitable life, otherwise it would not be eternal (John 3:16). Eternal life is life that lasts forever, and we have it now (John 3:36; see also John 5:24).

"My sheep hear my voice, and I know them, and they follow me" (John 10:37). Notice these three things. It matters not what profession a man makes, if he does not hear the voice of Christ he is not a Christian, and therefore the Saviour does not know him as His own. No matter what profession he may make, if he does not follow the Lord Jesus Christ he is only a sham and a hypocrite. He may follow for a while outwardly, such as those of whom the apostle Peter speaks: "But it is happened unto them according to the true proverb, The dog is turned to his own vomit again; and the sow that was washed to her wallowing in the mire" (II Peter 2:22). If that dog had ever been regenerated and become a sheep, and if that sow had ever been changed and become a lamb, neither would have gone back to the filth; but the dog was always a dog, and the sow was always a sow, and so went back to the old things. But the sheep of Christ are different. "They follow me," Jesus says; having a new birth, being born again, they receive a new life, and love to follow Jesus, otherwise they would not be Christians.

"My sheep hear my voice, and I know them, and they follow me; and I give them eternal life." How can a believer lose his life? It would not be eternal if it could be lost. "And they shall never perish, neither shall any man pluck them out of my hand." It is impossible, unthinkable that one who has eternal life can ever perish. "My Father, who gave them me, is greater than all; and no man is able to pluck them out of my Father's hand." Now I am in the hand of the Father and of the Son, and the devil himself cannot get me unless he can loosen those hands. Could there be any greater security? "Never perish . . . eternal life"—wondrous words! When you know you have eternal life, you will find your heart so filled with love that you will try to live for His glory.

Paul, in the Epistle to the Romans, is writing *to* believers when he asks, "Who shall separate us from the love of Christ?" and *of* believers when he answers that question in verses 38, 39: "For I am sure that neither death, nor life, nor angels, nor principalities, nor things present, nor things to come, nor powers, nor height, nor depth, nor anything else in all creation, will be able to separate us from the love of God in Christ Jesus our Lord" (R.S.V.). Nothing in death nor in life; surely this covers it all!

THE SPIRIT CONVICTS THE WORLD OF SIN— After the Lord Jesus left this earth the Holy Spirit came to "convince [convict] the world of sin and of righteousness and of judgment" (John 16:5-8). He did not come to convince the world of its unrighteousness, because of intemperance, because of hatreds, lasciviousness, covetousness, malice and other evil things which are rightfully classed as sinful. His purpose was not to convince men of sins but of *sin*. Every man who thinks at all knows that it is wrong to lie and steal and be intemperate and wicked; we all know these things, and if conscience becomes so numb by sinning against light, then God's holy law given at Sinai convinces of the sinfulness of such things as these. Then of what sin does the Holy Spirit come to convince? Notice, "Of sin, because they believe not in me." That is the great outstanding, damning sin which, if not repented of, is going to sink men to the depths of perdition for all eternity. Remember God's words: "He that believeth on him is not condemned: but he that believeth not is condemned already, because he hath not believed in the name of the only begotten Son of God" (John 3:18).

If the sinner stands, at last, condemned before the Almighty God, and hears Christ say, "Depart from me, I never knew you," it will not be simply because of the sins of his daily life. But the outstanding sin which will separate him from God forever will be that he has rejected the Saviour whom God has provided. He bore the iniquity of all upon the cross. It has often been said that the great question is not so much the sin question as the Son question; it is not so much what we have done as sinners, but how we respond to the fact that Christ has died as a ransom for sinners, and now God says, "What will you do with My Son?" If you trust Him, then the value of His atoning work goes over against your sins and iniquity; but if you refuse Him and turn away, then you must face God at last about your own sins; and the crowning sin of all will be that you rejected the Saviour who died to deliver you. "Of sin, because they believe not in me."

But notice that the Holy Spirit came also to convince the world of righteousness. "Of righteousness because I go to my Father, and ye see me no more." After He had completed the work of atonement God raised Him from the dead on the third day, and took Him up to His own right hand in Heaven. Sin put Jesus on the cross; righteousness put Him on the throne. And now, you need a righteousness which

He only can provide in order that you may stand before God uncondemned. You must have a righteousness which you cannot provide yourself. Christ Himself, exalted in Heaven, is the righteousness of all who put their trust in Him. The Spirit delights to point men, who are destitute of any righteousness of their own, to a seated Christ in Heaven, who is "made unto us righteousness."

"Of judgment, because the prince of this world is judged." When Satan stirred that crowd in Jerusalem to send the Lord Jesus to the cross, he sealed his own condemnation. At the cross Satan was judged by God, because of his attitude toward God's blessed Son, and the world has been judged in its prince. But now, through grace, all who trust in the Lord Jesus Christ have come out from under that judgment and are delivered from a world over which hangs the wrath of God; we are saved out of that world, which is what Peter meant when he said, "Save yourselves from this untoward generation."

FRUIT-BEARING—In John 15 there are three necessary provisions for a life that bears fruit: cleansing through the Word (vv. 2, 3); abiding in Christ (v. 4); keeping Christ's commandments (vv. 10, 12).

There are in like manner three progressive steps in fruit-bearing (1) *fruit* (v. 2); (2) *more fruit* (v. 2); (3) *much fruit* (vv. 5, 8); and in the bearing of much fruit the Father is glorified in the believer (v. 8). Fruit is spoken of in general in John 15, while Paul was privileged (Gal. 5:22, 23) to specifically give the name to nine fruits, "the fruit of the Spirit," and when such graces are possessed by the believer, the Father is glorified indeed.

APOSTASY—Apostasy, a "falling away." Apostasy differs from backsliding in that a true Christian may backslide, but an apostate was never born again. Judas Iscariot, never saved, was an apostate; Peter, a saved man, fell out of communion. The backslidden Christian loses his fellowship, joy, and fruitfulness, though not his salvation; for salvation is the free gift of God, including eternal life, and eternal security (John 5:24). An apostate is one who after professing to believe the gospel, turns away from and refutes his profession. The apostate is described in II Timothy 4:3, 4; and again in I John 2:19 (R.S.V.): "They went out from us, but they were not of us; for if they had been of us, they would have continued with us; but they went out, that it might be plain that they all are not of us." Their going out from us is a matter of doctrine. Though they may go on calling themselves Christians, they are not Christians; for apostates deny the fundamental doctrines concerning the person and work of Jesus Christ. "Whosoever transgresseth, and abideth not in the doctrine of Christ, hath not God. He that abideth in the doctrine of Christ, he hath both the Father and the Son. If there come any unto you, and bring not this doctrine, receive him not into your house, neither bid him God speed; for he that biddeth him God speed is partaker of his evil deeds" (II John 9-11).

FAITH AND WORKS CONTRASTED—It has been thought by some that a contradiction existed between what the Spirit of God inspired the apostle Paul to write in the Epistle to the Romans, and that which He also inspired James to write in the epistle bearing his name. There is no contradiction; the difference is this: in Romans we are told how a guilty sinner is justified by *faith* alone *before God*, whereas in James we are shown how the professed believer is justified by *works before men*. There should be no difficulty if this distinction is kept in view.

106

VEIL OF THE TEMPLE RENT—The veil of the temple (Matt. 27:51) separated the place where the priests entered from the Holy of Holies, and signified that no man could pass into the presence of God except the high priest once a year, on the day of atonement, and that "not without blood" (Heb. 9:1-10). But when Christ died as the propitiation for sin, that way into the Holy of Holies was opened up, and now God can come out in unhindered love for man; and man can go into God's presence, accepted in Christ. The veil was a symbol, a type of the body, the flesh of Christ (Heb. 10:20), and when that veil was rent (torn on the cross) it opened the "new and living way" into God's presence for believers.

THE GENEALOGY OF MARY—The first chapter of Matthew's Gospel contains what is undeniably the genealogy of Joseph, whose father was Jacob (v. 16). In the third chapter of Luke's Gospel is another genealogy where Joseph is called the son of Heli (or Eli) (v. 23). That the two genealogies cannot be of the same person is indisputable, as is the fact that it is impossible for Joseph to have two natural fathers. Now, in Matthew (1:11, 12), one of the lineage, through David's son Solomon, is Jechonias (another name for Coniah), who is barred with his descendants from ever occupying the throne of David (Jer. 22:30); this eliminates Matthew's genealogy from being the line of the Lord Jesus, who is the Heir to that throne, and must be so through direct descent. Therefore, the genealogy of the third chapter of Luke must be the one with Jesus' lineage, which cannot be through Joseph, as the Lord Jesus has no human father, and can only be through His mother Mary, He being the "seed of the woman" of Genesis 3:15; Luke's genealogy is unquestionably that of Mary, descended from another son of David, Nathan (v. 31), who is the full brother of Solomon (I Chron. 3:5); this avoids the line of Coniah (Jechonias). This would apparently make Heli the father-in-law of Joseph, confirmed by tradition, which also gives Ann as Mary's mother's name.

SCRIBES, PHARISEES AND SADDUCEES—Scribe (Gr. *grammateis*—writer). They were public writers to write at dictation, and to draw up legal documents. They were copiers of the Law and other parts of Scripture, and devoted themselves (1) to the study of the interpretation of the law, which was both civil and religious, and to determining its applications to daily life; their decisions becoming the oral law or tradition; (2) to the study of Scripture generally, regarding historical and doctrinal matters; (3) to teaching, each noted scribe having a company of disciples about him. Many were members of the Sanhedrin (Matt. 16:21; 26:3); though some believed in the Lord Jesus (Matt. 8:19), most were hopelessly prejudiced against Him (Matt. 21:15), and had a large share in the responsibility for His death. They were also associated in the persecutions of Peter and John (Acts 4:5, etc.), and in the martyrdom of Stephen (Acts 6:12). Public scribes still frequent the streets of cities of the Near East.

Pharisees (from Aramaic word meaning "separated"). A sect holding the doctrine of foreordination and considering it consistent with the free will of man. They believed in the immortality of the soul, in the resurrection, and in the existence of spirits; that men are rewarded or punished in the future life, according as they have lived in this life; that the souls of the wicked shall be held in prison forever under the earth, while those of the virtuous rise and live again (Acts 23:8). Pharisaism is the final result of that conception of religion which makes religion consist in conformity to the law, and promises God's grace only to the doers of the law. Religion becomes external, and the disposition of the heart less vital than the outward act. The interpretation of the law and its application to the details of ordinary life accordingly became a matter of grave consequence, expositions of the law growing to large bodies of precepts of binding force.

They also delivered to the people multitudinous observances, by succession from the fathers, which were not written in the law of Moses, these being the traditional interpretations of the elders which our Lord pronounced as being of no binding authority (Matt. 15:2, 3, 6). They were the worst persecutors of Jesus, and the objects of His scathing criticism (Matt. 23:13-29; Luke 11:42, 43).

Sadducees, a Jewish party and opponents of the Pharisees—few in number, but educated and usually wealthy. In distinction from the Pharisees they denied the resurrection (Matt. 22:23-33), the existence of angels and spirits (Acts 23:8), and placed no credence in the supernatural. They had members in the priesthood and the Sanhedrin.

EVIL (NOT SIN) CREATED BY GOD—

"I form the light, and create darkness; I make peace, and create evil. I the Lord do all these things" (Isa. 45:7).

The English word *evil* is so translated from the Hebrew word *ra*, also translated "sorrow, wretchedness, adversity, afflictions, calamities," but never translated *sin*. God created evil only in the sense that He made sorrow, wretchedness, etc., to be the sure fruits of sin.

THE ELEVEN MYSTERIES—As used in the New Testament, the "mysteries" are those truths which are now the common property of every believer, and no believer can properly enter upon the responsibilities flowing from the relationship in which he stands toward God, if he remains in ignorance of them. The eleven of most importance are: (1) the mysteries of the kingdom of Heaven (Matt. 13:3-50); (2) the mystery of Israel's blindness in the age of grace (Rom.

11:25 and context); (3) the mystery of the Rapture of the saints (I Cor. 15:51, 52; I Thess. 4:14-17); (4) the mystery of the true Church as embracing Jew and Gentile (Rom. 16:25; Eph. 3:1-11; 6:19; Col. 4:3); (5) the great mystery of Christ and the Church (Eph. 5:22-32); (6) the mystery of the indwelling Christ (Col. 1:26, 27); (7) the mystery of godliness, or piety (I Tim. 3:16); (8) the mystery of Christ, as the fullness of the Godhead embodied (Col. 2:2, 9); (9) the mystery of lawlessness (II Thess. 2:7; Matt. 13:33); (10) the mystery of the seven stars (Rev. 1:20); (11) the mystery of Babylon (Rev. 17:5, 7).

BACKSLIDER—SAVED OR LOST?—A backslidden Christian is still a Christian; is still a child of the Father, though out of fellowship. His condition is symbolized in the parable of the prodigal (Luke 15:11-32). Backsliding is attended by immeasurable loss; but salvation is a gift whose keeping is not committed to those who are saved. The same God who saves them, keeps them (see "Eternal Security"), all of which is illustrated in I Corinthians 11. In the latter part of that chapter there is a discussion of the disorderly conduct at the Lord's Supper by the Corinthian church; this had become so grievous that God had been compelled to exercise discipline by visiting His people with sickness and even death; for many of them had actually died under His hand. That is to say they were backslidden, and they died during their backsliding. And yet they went to Heaven as is shown by verses 30-32: "For this cause many are weak and sickly among you, and many sleep. For if we would judge ourselves, we should not be judged. But when we are judged, we are chastened of the Lord, that we should not be condemned with the world." Born-again Christians may backslide, but they can never lose their salvation. There is a vast difference between the backsliding of a believing Christian, and the apostasy of a mere professor. The apostate (described in I John 2:18, 19) goes out from us, but in so doing he proves that he was never of us.

LETTERS TO THE SEVEN CHURCHES—Revelation 1:20 tells us that the seven lampstands are the seven churches, and that there is a mystery connected with them; no solution to this mystery was found until some devout Scripture student went upon the assumption that God in the ensuing messages to the seven churches in Asia was giving us a prophetic history of the Church for this entire dispensation, and, upon comparison of the seven letters with Church history, it was found to work out perfectly.

(1) Ephesus (Rev. 2:1-7) pictures the Church as it was in the beginning, in the waning period of the apostolic age, when the Lord walked in the midst of His churches, His eyes upon everything there, to admonish, correct and control; in the beginning His name was the only center, and unto Him was the gathering of His saints. The Early Church walked in separation from the world. The word "Ephesus" means "desirable," such a term as a Greek would apply to the maiden of his choice.

(2) Smyrna (Rev. 2:8-11) depicts the Church in the persecution period, the first three hundred years. Smyrna means "myrrh," which is frequently used in Scripture in connection with the embalming of the dead. Myrrh had to be crushed to give out its fragrance, and so was the Church crushed under the iron heel of pagan Rome, giving out its fragrance to God in those years of almost constant martyrdom.

(3) Pergamum (Rev. 2:12-17) portrays the period of Church history from Constantine to the beginning of the papacy at the end of the sixth century A.D. The word Pergamum has two meanings, "marriage" and "elevation," and speaks of the time when the Church was elevated to a place

111

of power, and married to the world; when Church and state were united under Constantine and his successors.

(4) Thyatira (Rev. 2:18-28) pictures the Church during the papal period from the end of the sixth century to the sixteenth century A.D. The word Thyatira means "continual sacrifice." The significance of this is in the great fundamental error of the Church of Rome—the sacrifice of the Mass. Roman Catholic priests declare that in the Mass, they offer a continual sacrifice for the sins of the living and the dead, which is the central, the very root blasphemy, the denial of the *finished* work of the Lord Jesus Christ on Calvary's cross, the one and all-sufficient offering for the sins of a guilty world. Every time the priest stands at Rome's altar to offer the sacrifice of the Mass, he denies the unchanging efficacy of the work wrought by the Lord Jesus Christ upon the cross of Calvary.

(5) Sardis (Rev. 3:1-6) shows the reformation period from the sixteenth century A.D. Sardis means a "remnant" or "those who have escaped." The story is plain, and brings before us, prophetically, the great state churches of the Reformation, who escaped from Rome, only to fall eventually into cold, lifeless formalism.

(6) Philadelphia (Rev. 3:7-13) covers prophetically, the Protestant reawakening of the eighteenth and nineteenth centuries A.D. Philadelphia means "brotherly love," which implies that those contemplated here love as do brethren; and, as Sardis sets forth state churches of the Reformation, so Philadelphia sets forth those in Protestantism who emphasize the authority of the Word of God, and the preciousness of the name of Christ.

(7) Laodicea (Rev. 3:14-22) depicts the Church during the present time to the Lord's coming. Laodicea means "the rights of the people." What term more apt? This is the era

112

of democratization, both in the world and in the Church. The masses are realizing their power as never before; the terrific slogan, "Vox populi, vox Dei" (The voice of the people is the voice of God) is ringing throughout the world, and the spirit of this ultra-democratic age has invaded a large portion of the professed Church. The authority of God and His Word is rapidly being denied, hence the striking similarity between this letter to Laodicea and the latitudinarianism so prevalent about us. God says, "Because thou art lukewarm, and neither cold nor hot, I will spue thee out of my mouth." There is a great lack of burning zeal for His Word in the Church today, yet not an absolute repudiation of Christ and the Bible; instead, a nauseating indifference and lukewarm condition, abhorrent to the Spirit of God.

THE LAW OF MOSES—Israel received the Mosaic Covenant in three sections: (a) the commandments, the fundamental law of Israel, embodying the divine will (Exod. 20:1-26); (b) the judgments, covering Israel's social life (Exod. 21:1 to 24:11); (c) the ordinances, covering Israel's religious life (Exod. 24:12 to 31:18). As related to man dispensationally, the Mosaic law covered that period of time from Sinai to the crucifixion (Gal. 3:23, 24), and its relation to the believer during this age was made manifest by the legal teachings, especially regarding circumcision, as recorded in Acts 15:1-32 and Galatians 2:1-5.

Christian relationship is: God required righteousness under law (Exod. 19:5), but under grace counts all righteous who merely believe (Rom. 3:21, 22; 10:9, 10); the law is holy, just, good and also spiritual (Rom. 7:12-14), but man was unable to keep it, and it became a curse to him (Gal. 3:10), so Christ redeemed believers from that curse (Gal. 3:13), also redeeming them from under the law (Gal. 4:5) that they "might receive the adoption of sons"; and now believers, not only redeemed from the law, are also dead to it (Gal. 2:19), "being not under the law, but under grace" (Rom. 6:14).

CHRIST'S RELATION TO LAW OF MOSES—Christ was made (born) under the law (Gal. 4:4). He was sinless under the law (John 8:46). He expounded the law to the people, brushing off the traditional reasonings of the scribes and the Pharisees, and portraying it in its clear light to those who pretended to follow it (Luke 10:25-37). All the Old Testament types were fulfilled by Him, in Him, and in His crucifixion (Heb. 9:11-26). He redeemed us from the curse of the law, by becoming the curse for us; that in Him the blessings of the Abrahamic covenant might come also upon all the Gentiles who believed (Gal. 3:13, 14). Servants, slaves under the law, became sons and heirs merely by faith, having been redeemed by Him (Gal. 4:1-7). He "mediated a better covenant, the new covenant of grace (Heb. 8:6-13), and all believers, through Him, obtained access to that grace in which they stand (Rom. 5:2). And so was the "law of Christ" (John 13:34; Gal. 6:2) made known and put into effect, with its basis of love, actuated by the Holy Spirit in all believers.

BELIEVER DEAD TO THE LAW—Man formerly was (under law) the slave of sin, which led to death, but believers, under grace, have been freed from sin to become slaves of righteousness and of God, the return being eternal life in Christ Jesus (Rom. 6:16-23); the old self was crucified with Christ making the believer dead to sin and alive to God in Christ Jesus (Rom. 6:11).

Likewise, as in marriage (Rom. 7:1-6), when the husband dies the wife is freed from the marriage law, and as death frees her from the husband, so crucifixion with Christ frees the believer from the law; "he has died to the law through the body of Christ" (v. 4).

THE PASSOVER—The Passover (Exod. 12:1-28) is a type of Christ (John 1:29, 36). The lamb of sacrifice must be without blemish or spot (Exod. 12:5; I Peter 1:19). In order to prove it, it was to be kept up four days (Exod. 12:3, 6); in like manner the Lord Jesus was proven before His enemies (John 7:46; 8:46; 18:38). The lamb must be killed, the blood shed (Exod. 12:6; Heb. 9:22); the blood upon the houses was the guarantee of safety, of the "pass over" (Exod. 12:13). It was typical of the protection of the shed blood of Christ; the feast of the Passover itself was typical of Christ through the Supper of Mark 14:22-25, each of which were to be observed, the former by the Jews as a memorial of their release from bondage in Egypt (Exod. 12:14), the latter as a memorial to the Lord Jesus Christ (Luke 22:19).

MELCHIZEDEK—TYPE OF CHRIST—Melchizedek, king of righteousness and king of peace (Heb. 7:2), king of Salem and priest of the Most High God (Gen. 14:18, ff.). By Salem, Jerusalem is probably meant, for (1) the city was in existence, bore the name of Jerusalem, and was under a king before the conquest of Canaan by the Israelites. (2) The name Jerusalem means city or, to the Hebrew ear, foundation of peace or safety, so that Salem is an appropriate abbreviation. (3) Salem is named for the name of Jerusalem in Psalm 76:2. (4) The comparison of David's Lord with Melchizedek in Psalm 110:4 appears most apt if Melchizedek was king of the same city as was David. (5) Jerusalem is on the route from Hobah and Damascus to Hebron, whither Abraham was going.

Melchizedek, as described in Hebrews 5:10; 6:20; and in chapter 7, was without father, without mother, without genealogy. This statement means that his pedigree was not recorded (cf. Ezra 2:59, 62). He is further described as having neither beginning of days nor end of life, of whom it is testified that he lives. He suddenly emerges from the unknown and as suddenly disappears; it is not known whence he came nor whither he went; neither birth nor death is assigned to him; he is a type of undying priesthood. Melchizedek came forth from his royal city to welcome the returning benefactor of the peoples of Canaan, and Abraham recognized him as a priest of the true God, and publicly testified to sharing the same or a kindred faith by paying tithes to him who was representative of the Most High God, to the priest who had ascribed the victory to the Creator of Heaven and earth (cf. Acts 10:35).

The author of the Epistle to the Hebrews shows how great a personage Melchizedek was, to whom even Abraham, and through him virtually Levi, paid tithes, thus admitting their inferiority. When thus our Lord was made a high priest after the order of Melchizedek, He held a far higher office than the Aaronic priesthood.

JUDGMENTS OF BELIEVERS—Three types of judgments for believers are to be distinguished in the New Testament:

(1) The judgment of sins. On Calvary's cross, according to God's reckoning, the Lord Jesus Christ, substituting for man, died for man's sins, so that all who have believed unto salvation will never come into judgment for sins (John 5:24, R.V.; II Cor. 5:19-21; Gal. 3:13).

(2) The judgment of self. This is the believer's judgment of himself for his own sinning, and should go on constantly. When the children of God judge themselves, when they confess their sins, they are freely forgiven; but failure to do so

116

brings chastening (I Cor. 5:1-5; 11:31, 32; II Cor. 2:5-7; Heb. 12:7; I John 1:9).

(3) The judgment of believers' works, which will be at the judgment seat of Christ, at His second coming, to determine not salvation but rewards for good works (II Cor. 5:10; I Cor. 3:11-15).

THE FINAL JUDGMENT—The judgment of the Great White Throne (Rev. 20:11-15), and of the "dead" (v. 12). The resurrection of the saved precedes this by one thousand years (Rev. 20:5); here we have a picture of the second resurrection; the "dead," as mentioned, are undeniably the lost, the great multitude of the unsaved from Adam to the time now held in view. The dead, "small and great," stand before the throne and are judged from their records in the "books," according to their works (v. 12), and if their names are not found in the book of life they are cast into the lake of fire for all eternity (v. 13).

INSPIRATION OF SCRIPTURE—"All scripture is given by inspiration of God" (II Tim. 3:16). The testimony is not that the writers were inspired, but the writings; and the writings are made up of words and the letters which form the words. Therefore, the words are inspired, or God-breathed, including every inflection of the words and every little particle. This must be so from the nature of the case: if only the thoughts were inspired, and they were left to chance selection of words which weak, fallible, and sometimes illiterate, men might choose, it is obvious that we have no revelation at all. We can get at the thoughts of others only through their words; if the words of the Scriptures were not the precisely prepared and suitable vehicle for the transmission of the thoughts of the writers, so far as we are concerned, the inspired thoughts would be of no value whatsoever. Fortu-

117

nately, however, we are not left to human reasoning to settle this question. It is the declaration of the Bible concerning all the Old Testament prophets and writers that "men spake from God, being moved by the Holy Spirit" (II Peter 1:21, R.V.). It is not that they thought, but that they spoke as they were moved by the Spirit, often indeed uttering thoughts, the significance and scope of which they themselves did not understand, and often using words contrary to their own natural will and purpose, as may be seen from Numbers 22:35-38; I Samuel 19:20-24; I Kings 13:11-22; John 11:49-52.

SCRIPTURE EXACTNESS—

And he stood up to read; and there was given to him the book of the prophet Isaiah. He opened the book and found where it was written,

"The Spirit of the Lord is upon me, because he has anointed me to preach good news to the poor. He has sent me to proclaim release to the captives and recovering of sight to the blind, to set at liberty those who are oppressed, to proclaim the acceptable year of the Lord."

And he closed the book, and gave it back to the attendant, and sat down (Luke 4:16-20, R.S.V.).

The passage quoted above is from the Old Testament (Isa. 61:1, 2) and is an outstanding example of the meticulous exactness of Scripture. Our Lord did not finish reading the passage, but stopped at a comma after "the acceptable year of the Lord," which is still going on, and has been for over nineteen hundred years. The end of the sentence is "and the day of vengeance of our God"; Jesus did not read that because the day of God's vengeance has not yet come, but it may commence at any moment, when the Lord Jesus descends from Heaven with a shout, with the voice of the archangel and the trump of God (I Thess. 4:16).

118

THE SUBJECT AND PURPOSE OF THE BIBLE—
God the Creator has revealed Himself, His purpose, and His
will to man in various ways: through nature (Rom. 1:20),
in Christ (Gal. 4:4), and through the Bible, the written
Word of God.

(1) Its purpose. The one supreme purpose, as we understand it from the written Word of God, which actuates God
in everything, is the *glory of God*. From the human viewpoint
this would seem self-seeking, but this theme cannot be lim-
ited to the range of human conceptions. We must conclude
from Scripture revelation, that because God is infinite in
His being, His perfections, and His blessedness, He is worthy
of infinite glory, and it would be infinite injustice should His
creation withhold from Him that honor and glory which are
rightfully His.

God is not self-seeking. He as the fountain source of all
truth must be true to Himself as Creator and Lord of all.
It is man who is self-centered, and who can conceive of nothing more desirable than that man should be exalted and glorified; who does not understand the relation that should exist
between the Creator and the creature; and does not ascribe
to the Creator that glory which is rightfully due Him, because of His person, His character, and His position (Exod.
24:10; I Chron. 16:17-29; Ps. 57:11; Isa. 6:1).

Therefore, the supreme purpose of the Bible is that He may
be glorified. "All things . . . that are in heaven, and that are
in the earth, visible and invisible, whether they be thrones,
or dominions, or principalities, or powers: all things were
created by him and for him" (Col. 1:16); angels and men, the
material universe, and every creature, all created for His
glory. "The heavens declare the glory of God" (Ps. 19:1).
The nation Israel is for God's glory (Jer. 13:11; Isa. 43:7,
21, 25; 60:1, 3, 21). Salvation is unto His glory (Rom. 9:23).

119

Even the believer's death is said to be to this one end (John 21:19; Phil. 1:20).

(2) Its subject. The Lord Jesus Christ is the supreme subject of the Bible; like a glass this Book reflects "the glory of the Lord" (II Cor. 3:18); but the Lord Himself has been manifested that He, in turn, might reflect the glory of God. "For God, who commanded the light to shine out of darkness, hath shined in our hearts, to give the light of the knowledge of the glory of God in the face of Jesus Christ" (II Cor. 4:6).

THE HEAVENLY CITIZENSHIP—The passage of Hebrews 12:22-24 enumerates only incidentally (for the purpose of the passage is a contrast between law and grace) the classes composing the heavenly citizenship. These are three: (1) "an innumerable company of angels"; (2) "the general assembly and church of the first-born"; and (3) "the spirits of just [justified] men made perfect." The first class includes the supernatural intelligences who have not sinned; the second, the saved of this dispensation between the first and second advents of Christ; the third, all other redeemed ones in preceding dispensations from Adam to Christ, and all future redeemed ones in the Great Tribulation and the Millennium.

THE GREAT TRIBULATION—The Great Tribulation is that time of unparalleled anguish that comes upon the world (Rev. 3:10). The Jews, however, will be the chief sufferers; it is the "time of Jacob's trouble" (Jer. 30:7). It will last for three and one-half years, corresponding to the last half of the seventieth week of Daniel's prophecy (Dan. 9:24-27; Rev. 11:2, 3). It begins when the completed Church is caught up to meet the Lord in the air (I Thess. 4:14-18). The Man of Sin, called the "prince that is to come" in Daniel

9:26, the "beast out of the sea" of Revelation 13:1, during his cruel reign, will enter into an alliance with the Jews; but will break that covenant after three and one-half years, forbidding further worship of Jehovah and demanding that he himself be worshiped as God (Matt. 24:15). Multitudes will turn to God during that terrible period of judgment (Rev. 7:9-14). Satan will be for a while unceasingly active (Rev. 12:12), aided by an innumerable host of demons (Rev. 9:2-11). The coming of the Lord Jesus Christ in glory (Matt. 24:29, 30) will put an end to this terrible time of suffering on earth, when He establishes the promised kingdom, restoring the throne of David, and reigning thereon for a thousand years as King of kings and Lord of lords.

THE ANTICHRIST—The Antichrist is a person, not to be confused with the "many antichrists" of I John 2:18, nor the "spirit of antichrist" of I John 4:3. He is the "beast out of the earth" (Rev. 13:11-18), the "false prophet" (Rev. 16: 13; 19:20; 20:10), and the "man of sin" or "lawless one" (II Thess. 2:3, 4, 6, 8); and will be the last religious head of the Jewish people, but will not be manifested until the Rapture of the Church, when the Holy Spirit, who is the "restrainer" of II Thessalonians 2:7, will be gone.

WORKING OUT OUR OWN SALVATION—The expression "work out your own salvation," as used by the apostle Paul (Phil. 2:12) does not refer to salvation as to the believer's eternal welfare. This is evident when it is recalled that the epistle is addressed to those *who are already saved*, to the "saints in Christ Jesus" (Phil. 1:1). The word "salvation" in 1:19 evidently relates to Paul's hope of being delivered from prison and permitted to visit his Philippian friends—in fact, the word is translated "deliverance" in the Revised Standard Version, which is a perfectly good translation of this Greek word for "salvation." In Philippians 2:12 it undoubtedly signifies "deliverance," in the sense that the Philippian believers should work out their *own deliverance* with fear and trembling, in solving their own problems; though Paul was not with them to help, *God* was there, even dwelling in and with them, and working among them.

THE TWENTY-FOUR ELDERS—It is conceded that the twenty-four "elders" of Revelation 4 stand for the Church. It must always be remembered in interpreting the Revelation that it is a book in which truth is revealed by signs, or symbols. The "elders" are redeemed (v. 9); are royal and priestly (v. 10), and are twenty-four in number, which is significant of priesthood, as David divided the priests into four and twenty courses. In Revelation 1:6 the quality of kingship and function of priesthood are spoken of in connection with the Church. Again, all through the book, it is noticeable that the elders have the secret of things, as for example, Revelation 5:5; 7:13, 14; which accords with John 15:15. The Scriptures give no hint of any other body of saints of whom all these things are true.

FALLING FROM GRACE—There is no such thing for born-again persons as losing their salvation, or "falling from grace." The only reference in the Bible to falling from grace is in Galatians 5:4, where Paul declares that those who were turning to law works for saving them or keeping them had "fallen from grace." It is an error to apply this expression in any other way.

WHEN DID THE WISE MEN OF THE EAST SEE JESUS?—Only Matthew 2 tells of the visit of the Magi, the Wise Men from the East; Herod's rage, and the massacre of the innocents at Bethlehem; the flight into Egypt, and the return therefrom after Herod's death.

These events quite evidently did not occur at the very time of Jesus' birth, but some time afterward, for Luke states in chapter 2 of his Gospel that, following His birth and circumcision, Joseph and Mary brought Him up to Jerusalem from Bethlehem to present Him to the Lord, and that when they had performed everything according to the law of the Lord, *they returned to Nazareth*, their own city in Galilee, where the child grew and became strong. "Now his parents went to Jerusalem every year to the feast of the Passover," Luke points out in verse 41, and evidently they remained at Nazareth some twelve months, or until the time for the next feast of the Passover at Jerusalem, when they took the young child to Jerusalem, about eighty-eight miles south of Nazareth, and during the Passover time remained, quite naturally, in Bethlehem, as it was their ancestral city, and only five miles from Jerusalem. Matthew relates that immediately after the visit of the Magi from the East "when they had departed," Joseph was warned to flee into Egypt. "And he arose and took the young Child and His mother by night and departed into Egypt, and was there until the death of Herod." Therefore, the visit of the Magi to Bethlehem, and the flight into Egypt from Bethlehem must have occurred when the Child Jesus was at least a year old. The shepherds in Luke found Jesus as "a Babe wrapped in swaddling clothes," the Wise Men in Matthew as a "young Child with His mother." The shepherds found Him in the stable of the inn, lying in a manger, the Wise Men found Him in a "house." This view also explains why Herod destroyed all children in Bethlehem *up to two years old,* in seeking the life of the new-born King. Confusion has been caused by the translation of the first verse of Matthew 2, the King James

Version making it read "Now when Jesus was born in Bethlehem of Judea in the days of Herod the king, behold there came wise men from the east to Jerusalem," and the American Standard Version is of no help; but the best rendering for clarity is perhaps Weymouth's: "Now after the birth of Jesus, which took place in Bethlehem of Judea in the reign of Herod the king, there came to Jerusalem certain Magi from the east," etc.

Had the star, seen in the East by the Wise Men, first appeared at the time of Jesus' birth, they could not possibly have reached Judea a few days later, in view of the primitive methods of travel, and the great distance involved. It seems certain from all information, that their arrival in Jerusalem was at the time of the Passover, one year after our Lord's birth. The star did not lead them all the way from their eastern home, verse 9 seeming to imply that upon leaving Herod and starting for Bethlehem, the star "which they saw in the east" reappeared to them.

The number of only three Wise Men was most certainly incorrect, and was probably suggested by the three kinds of gifts, gold, frankincense, and myrrh; it seems reasonable to believe that there was a far larger number, a number which was large enough to startle Jerusalem, and bring trouble into the heart of its wicked king, Herod; picture them in a great procession through the streets of Jerusalem, asking in vain the question, "Where is He that hath been born King of the Jews?" There was no answer—the great city had no knowledge of that King.

DAY OF CHRIST; DAY OF THE LORD; DAY OF GOD—The "day of Christ" is related to the Rapture of I Thessalonians 4:14-18, and the events transpiring in Heaven immediately following that event—the judgment of believers' works, the Marriage Supper of the Lamb, etc. (I Cor. 1:8; 5:5; II Cor. 1:14; Phil. 1:6, 10; 2:16). The expression "day of Christ" occurs in II Thessalonians 2:2 in the Authorized Version, but this is an error in translation which the Revised Version and Revised Standard Version rightly correct to the "day of the Lord."

The "day of the Lord" is an expression frequently found in the Old Testament, and the New Testament has it in Acts 2:20 (quoted from Joel 2:31); I Thessalonians 5:2; II Thessalonians 2:2 (R.V. and R.S.V.); II Peter 3:10. It is also called "that day" and "the great day." It begins with the second coming of Christ (not the Rapture, which is His descending into the air *for* His saints, but His coming to earth *with* them after the great tribulation) and extends through the Millennium.

The "day of God" is the end and consummation of the "day of the Lord" (II Peter 3:10-13; cf. I Cor. 15:24).

THE FULLNESS OF THE GENTILES—The fullness of the Gentiles is an expression referring to the people to be gathered out from the Gentiles for the Lord's name in this present dispensation (Acts 15:14). This people from among the Gentiles being united with the remnant according to the election of grace gathered out from Israel, constitute the true Church.

Believing Jews and Gentiles are thus united by the blood of Christ, "Who hath made both one, and hath broken down the middle wall of partition between us; having abolished in his flesh the enmity, even the law of commandments contained in ordinances; for to make in himself of twain one new man, so making peace" (Eph. 2:14, 15).

When this body of Christ shall have been completed, then the "fullness of the Gentiles" will have come in; after this,

God will take up Israel again, the Lord Jesus Christ will return in His second coming, and will turn away ungodliness from Jacob, which is His covenant with them, when He shall take away their sins (Rom. 11:25-27). And then shall come the Millennium, the universal blessing that the world awaits. "He shall cause them that come of Jacob to take root; Israel shall blossom and bud, and fill the face of the world with fruit" (Isa. 27:6).

CONSECRATION—Consecration, yieldedness. "Yield yourselves [the ego, selfhood, inner self, including spirit and soul] unto God . . . and your members as instruments of righteousness unto God" (Rom. 6:13).

This yieldedness is (1) an act (Rom. 12:1, 2), and (2) a state—"yet not I" (Gal. 2:20); "always bearing about in the body the death of the Lord Jesus" (II Cor. 4:10). The definite *act* of yielding is the beginning of a *state* of yieldedness. That is consecration. If the state of yieldedness is departed from by a lapse into self-will, the remedy is *not* "reconsecration" (of which Scripture knows nothing), but *confession*.

"THE KENOSIS"

Have this mind among yourselves, which you have in Christ Jesus, who, though he was in the form of God, did not count equality with God a thing to be grasped, but emptied himself, taking the form of a servant, being born in the likeness of men. And being found in human form he humbled himself and became obedient unto death, even death on a cross (Phil. 2:5-8, R.S.V.).

The title comes from the Greek expression which means "emptied himself" or "divested himself," and is rendered in our King James Version "made himself of no reputation."

The Lord Jesus Christ existed from all eternity in the form

126

of God, which is a declaration of His true Deity. No mere creature could exist in the form of God. Lucifer aspired to this, and for his impiety was hurled down from the archangel's throne. Our Lord Jesus Christ was in the full enjoyment of this by right, because He was the Eternal Son. He thought equality with God not a thing to be held on to or grasped. Equal with God He was, but He chose to take the place of subjection and lowliness. He chose to step down from that sublime height which belonged to Him, even "the glory which He had with the Father before the world was," and took the servant's form to do the Father's will.

The first man aspired to be as God and fell. The second man, the Lord from Heaven, came from the Godhead's fullest glory down to Calvary's depths of woe. He did not retain the outward semblance of Deity, but relinquished His rightful position to become the Saviour of sinners. To do this He emptied Himself, divested Himself, of His divine prerogatives.

Let there be no mistake as to this. While we reverently draw near to behold this great sight, let us accept the declaration of Holy Scripture in all its fullness. He divested Himself of something, but of what? Not of His Deity, for that could not be. He was ever the Son of the Father, and, as such, a divine Person. He could take manhood into union with Deity, but He could not cease to be divine. Of what, then, did He divest Himself? Surely of His rights as God the Son. He chose to come to this earth to take a place of subjection, took upon Himself the form of a servant, and was made in the likeness of man.

Observe the distinction brought out in these two verses. He existed from eternity in the form of God, and came here to take the form of a servant. Angels are servants, but "surely it is not with angels he is concerned" (Heb. 2:16, R.S.V.). He became in the likeness of men, and it was all voluntary on His part. As a man on earth He chose to be guided by the Holy Spirit, and daily received from the Father, through the Word of God, the instruction which it became Him, as a Man, to receive. His mighty works of power were not wrought by His own divine omnipotence alone, for He chose that they should be wrought in the power of the Holy Spirit. This is the marvelous and important doctrine of the Kenosis, as revealed in Scripture in contrast to the false teaching of men.

Men have added to this what Scripture does *not* say. They have declared that when He came to earth, He ceased to be God; that He became but an ignorant Galilean peasant. Hence His knowledge of divine mysteries was no greater than what might have been expected of any other good man of His day and generation. Therefore His testimony of Scripture has no real weight. He did not know more than others of His day knew. He was not competent to speak as to the authors of the Old Testament books. He thought Daniel wrote the book that bears his name, and that Moses penned the Pentateuch. But the wiseacres of today do not hesitate to declare that He was wrong, and they base their declaration on the position above taken. He emptied Himself of His divine knowledge, they say, therefore He could not speak with authority.

CONTENTS

and I have trouble locating bulls. Can
anyone help me solve this problem?

What pre-hunt preparations should one
or two hunters make if they won't have an
ATV or horses to pack out the meat?

How can you hunt bulls when they stay
up all night rutting and feeding and quit
talking by 8 a.m.?

If I had to spend a night in the woods,
what would you say are the most important things to have with me to make sure
I survive?

What's the best tool for field-dressing an
elk or other big game animal? I've heard of
a guy quartering an elk with a Leatherman,
and I imagine if you bone out your meat it
can be done with just a knife. But what if
you want to take out the rack? You need a
saw or hatchet, don't you?

In many articles on hunting, the authors
talk about walking miles before sunrise

to get to their hunting territory. How do they see where they are going? What kind of light source do they use? I'd appreciate any tips about hiking to a hunting spot in the dark.

Is there an effective rule of thumb to determine when elk will come to water to drink?

Do elk perceive the sounds of an ATV as benign? Do they learn to associate them with danger? Is there a point at which an ATV becomes a liability rather than an asset in elk hunting?

When an elk is killed in warm weather in remote country with only walk-in access, and it will take a couple of days to pack it out, what is the best way to preserve the meat? How can you tell if the meat is spoiled?

I often face one- to two-hour climbs before daylight in freezing weather to reach prime elk hunting locations. I'd like to know how other hunters avoid, or manage, overheating during a strenuous climb.

INTRODUCTION

"What's the most important thing for a first-time elk hunter to know?"

In this book you'll find a passel of answers to that question—enough solid advice from experienced elk hunters to catapult a newcomer to the head of the class. Even a crusty veteran with fifty notches on his elk stick is likely to pick up something new and useful to tuck away for future reference, just from that one set of answers. With twenty more questions and over 170 more pieces of advice (all sound, but some maybe just a bit smart-alecky) available in this book, I'd advise anyone seeking elk hunting know-how to keep on reading.

Members of the Rocky Mountain Elk Foundation—experienced hunters from all across North America, with headquarters in the heart of elk country, Missoula, Montana—have been answering our fellow hunters' most pressing questions about elk and elk hunting since 2004, when we introduced our Elk Hunting Q&A department in *Bugle* magazine. We've had room in the magazine for about half the answers we've received, and stockpiled the rest.

Here, for the first time, you'll find the complete trove in one handy volume.

There's no end to new knowledge, new experiences, and new insights about elk and elk hunting. You learn something new almost every day you're out there after them. Some days you come away with more questions than answers. This book will go a long way to reducing any elk-knowledge deficit you might be experiencing.

In answer to that first-time elk hunter question, RMEF member John Wallace of Vancouver, Washington, advises novices to go with somebody who knows what he or she is doing. Wallace also recommends books by recognized elk hunting experts Jim Zumbo, Don Laubach, and Mark Henckel. "But," he adds, "the best [information] appear[s] in the Elk Foundation's *Bugle* magazine, in the form of letters and articles from other hunters."

That's what we like to hear. For almost a quarter of a century, members of the Rocky Mountain Elk Foundation have been sharing elk hunting stories, thoughts, and wisdom in the pages of our magazine. Besides reading *Bugle*, the next-best way to get yourself closer to the honey hole of consistent elk hunting success is to read this book.

Don Burgess, *Bugle* hunting editor

Shooting a bull in its bed means you did a lot of things right. What is the most important factor in catching a bull with his guard down?

Dan Crockett
Missoula, Montana

• • •

To successfully take a bedded bull elk, you must beat his nose. Of the three senses that comprise a bull's defenses—sight, hearing, and smell—smell is the one he will trust unfailingly.

You can fool his eyesight by wearing appropriate camo, moving slowly, taking advantage of natural cover, and using a good pair of binoculars. Beat his hearing by wearing quiet clothing (wool/fleece) that doesn't make unnatural sounds, moving with a slow, irregular pace, and cow-calling occasionally.

To beat a bull's nose you can use any combination of the popular scent-control clothing or sprays, commercial cover scents, or naturally occurring scents like pine or sage, and stepping in elk wallows or droppings. But most important: play the wind. In the mountains the air is seldom calm. In addition to thermals and storm fronts, slight and fickle breezes swirl most days. Use a small squeeze bottle of unscented talc or a small feather tied to a bow or rifle barrel to constantly monitor air currents.

I've hunted elk and guided elk hunters for the past twenty-five years in Wyoming, Montana, and Colorado and been lucky enough to take three elk in their beds. I won't mention the number of times I heard one go or saw a flash of antler or hide making a clean getaway.

Dave Engelhardt
Waverly, Iowa

• • •

Of primary importance is to be scent-free. Follow this advice, which is older than our forefathers: "Always keep the wind in your face and the sun at your back." Next, use every bit of natural terrain to remain inconspicuous. It helps to be as familiar as possible with the bull's natural habits and habitat. Whether or not a kill is made, finding a bull in its bed is the thrill of a lifetime.

Kale B. Barb
Harrisonburg, Virginia

• • •

If you hunt where elk bed in the dark timber, you might benefit from trying this tactic I discovered on my last bowhunt. After getting into a calling match with a very responsive bull across the creek, I arranged to have my hunting partner Mark keep the bull bugling. Meanwhile, I was able to follow the sound until I spotted the beautiful 5x5 bedded down just beyond my bow range. From there I closed the distance to thirty yards, before spooking him in the process of nocking an arrow. Disregarding the final outcome, the plan worked remarkably well for at least three reasons: (1) the bull was distracted by

Mark's consistent challenge calls; (2) thanks to his vocal assistance, it wasn't just a shot in the dark to try and find him; (3) after I spotted him, I was able to make intelligent decisions on how to make my approach.

Jon Klacik
Grand Junction, Colorado

• • •

The answer, in my opinion, is to work from above the elk with a great deal of patience. I have had the good fortune to do this once with a rifle and once with a muzzleloader.

Roger Dienert
Hankinson, North Dakota

• • •

I have been lucky enough to do this three times. The common denominators are:

1. Snow, to soften footsteps.
2. No wind.
3. Mid-afternoon. I believe they sleep more soundly in afternoon than morning.
4. Mid-week. This relates to weekend hunting pressure on public land.
5. Wearing quiet clothing.

6. A bedding area that is relatively constant in elevation with sight lines of at least twenty yards.
7. Lots of luck.

Greg Schriner
Thornton, Colorado

• • •

I have hunted elk for over thirty years, and during the day when I am hunting on foot or at a stand I will occasionally work on the cow call. This seems to put the bull at ease, for it's a sound he associates with a cow elk moving through the woods.

Donald Schrader
Nashville, Tennessee

• • •

Most definitely, the single most important factor is to approach from downwind. The second biggest factor is knowing where the bull elk is bedded. Unfortunately, the only bedded elk in a five-square-mile area of steep, heavily forested country might be in a patch of timber or park no bigger than your living room. If you move through elk country at the very slow, stealthy pace necessary to creep up on a bull elk, you may grow old and die before you reach the right park or timber patch. The best advice I can give in this regard is to buy the best-quality spotting scope that you can afford and use it religiously until you find a bull in his bed. Close the distance as fast as you can until you think you're within several hundred yards of him, and then start your extremely slow, deliberate upwind approach.

John Flynn
Townsend, Montana

• • •

I killed a mature 5x6 bull at forty-eight yards in his bed in heavy timber. He was with several cows. I was never detected. I feel these three factors are most important:

1. Keep the wind in your face.
2. Move slowly and quietly.
3. Keep searching intently.

Gerald Shopp
Redding, California

• • •

Imagine the elk are hunting you. Whoever spots the other one first wins. Take a step and look for five minutes, then look for another five minutes as you have probably underestimated the first five minutes.

Elk will often bed with a view of the valley below them. One of the best spectator sports elk enjoy is watching hunters climbing a hill. I have often found myself leaning against a tree out of breath and sweating and hearing an elk say "Yuk Yuk Yuk." To avoid being laughed at you should stalk them from above.

Michael Cox
Estes Park, Colorado

QUESTION **2**

Is there any point in pursuing elk that have been spooked and are moving away from you? Is there a way to get a second chance at them?

Dennis Tandberg
Harlowton, Montana

• • •

I've had second chances at spooked elk by waiting an hour and then slowly following the tracks. There's one U-shaped Montana ridge, bounded by a river on one side with cliffs on another and clear-cuts to the east and north, where I've caught up to bands as often as three times in a day. When pushed, those elk turn big circles, very similar to white-tailed deer.

If you carry a pack and sleep on the track, you can pursue elk long and far. It pays to leave the tracks occasionally and circle. You might get the drop on elk that are watching their back trail.

Keith McCafferty
Bozeman, Montana

• • •

My comrades and I here in the Pacific Northwest have often spooked elk in the morning and found them a few hours later feeding in a clear-cut or quiet glade. I have found that older bulls like their special places and will return to their lairs faithfully day after day. This does not make them easy to get, for their rainforest homes are a labyrinth of hiding places. But do not despair if one runs from you. He might just circle back and try to get a look at you without you seeing him.

David Brooks
Copalis, Washington

• • •

If you hurry to a vantage point, you might spot your spooked elk moving up the next sidehill, crossing a bottom, or topping out over a ridge, still within range. Judicious use of a cow call will sometimes calm or stop them long enough for you to get another opportunity.

Fred Benton
Mount Shasta, California

• • •

Elk can be single-minded, capable of amazing tunnel vision. I once watched a lone coyote stampede a trio of cow elk away from a high country spring. Sudden movement by wild turkeys at the perimeter of the treeline spun the fugitives yet again. The poor coyote felt like a misguided rush-hour commuter going the wrong direction on the freeway. On crowded public lands, hunters may redirect running elk multiple times in a matter of minutes, so it pays to stay alert after you've spooked some.

David Regela
El Paso, Texas

• • •

If the lead cow has your scent, you might as well chase a tornado. If, however, the bull of your dreams is in the herd, circle downwind, stay out of sight, anticipate where the herd is headed, and get there in a hurry! Never follow directly behind, because elk check their back trail often.

Blane Gilliland
Riverton, Wyoming

• • •

I have watched spooked elk run for miles in semi-open terrain, especially when they have been repeatedly harassed by hunters. But when moderately disturbed, they may only go to the next patch of good security habitat.

Watch the direction they go, give them a couple of hours, then follow without getting upwind of them. When you find that they've entered some good security habitat, circle downwind and gradually close in.

Greg Munther
Missoula, Montana

• • •

It is usually best to back off and try again another day, but not always. You still have a chance on animals that are nervously moving off but aren't sure why. A nervous herd is often vocal, and this will enable you to keep track of them as you parallel the herd downwind and out of sight.

Remain silent, because calling will key them in on your location. If you can get out in front of the herd, or in front of an animal that is straggling behind the herd, you may be able to set up an effective ambush. I have taken two elk in recent years using this strategy.

Tony Pettis
Newport, Oregon

• • •

Elk don't want to break cover unless they truly feel in danger. I don't think they really get alarmed until they smell a hunter, and then it's adios. After all, they hear and see movement in the timber from a variety of animals, including other elk.

Last fall I spotted a bull on a distant ridge. The snow was crunchy during my approach, and he heard me but did not see or smell me. He spooked from his bed, trotted off about 300 yards, and bedded down again in a nearby thicket. Elk will often bed so they can watch their back trail. Wolves, lions, and bears usually come in on the tracks, because that is where the scent is and predators hunt by smell. I changed my approach and was able to sneak in and kill the nice 6x6.

Cody Hensen
Philipsburg, Montana

• • •

My answer applies to rifle hunting in areas with few elk and no other hunters. Once you spook elk, the only way I know to get a second chance is to get on their track and walk them down. You'll need to be in good shape, have good tracking snow, and most of the day to do it. If you got on the track in the morning, by late afternoon there's a good chance you'll catch 'em going up the other side of a ravine or canyon. I'd rather track them for a while, figure out where they're headed, and catch them there the next day.

Gary Edinger
Kennan, Wisconsin

QUESTION 3

Where I hunt here in the Pacific Northwest, an open area is anywhere you can stand in one place and wave your arms without hitting a bush or tree. Any ideas on how to hunt elk in this part of the country?

Jerry Pfeifer
Issaquah, Washington

• • •

Sneaking along and stopping to glass every other step is the best bet, while always keeping the wind in your favor. You are not going to see a whole elk in thick timber; look for horizontal back lines, the twitch of an ear, the gleam of an antler, an odd patch of color. Also, pay attention to game trails in the area. Elk don't like to wade through the brush any more than we do. They will use established game trails, and a hunter can set up an ambush near a trail.

Cody Hensen
Philipsburg, Montana

• • •

Living in northwestern Montana, I know the frustration of crawling around on steep, brushy mountainsides littered with blowdowns and feeling as if I'm looking for a needle in a haystack. But here are a few things I find helpful:

1. Know the area you are hunting. Elk will be found in small bands. Scout thoroughly and try to determine if the elk follow a pattern.
2. Avalanche chutes may hold elk during the night. If they're not there at first light, study the sign to see if they were there and try to figure out where they went. They may be closer than you think.
3. If you jump elk, you'll know it: they will make a tremendous amount of noise. Feel free to run toward the noise. In the

confusion they're as apt to run into you as away from you.

4. In thick cover a rifle scope can be a liability. After jumping more than one bull at less than twenty yards, I went back to using iron sights.

Aaron Klug
Columbia Falls, Montana

• • •

In the rain forests west of the Cascade Mountains, most of the old-growth timber has been cut, and most timberlands where elk now live are logged regularly. Elk like the clear-cuts, and you can often find them there, especially in the early morning. When the elk leave the clear-cuts you may follow them through the forest, but you will usually not see them again until they enter another clear-cut.

I love hunting the old-growth, where I can find it. It's very open under the taller trees, almost as good as clear-cuts for seeing and shooting. Elk mostly hide in the forest but prefer the openings for feeding. My hunting brings me in and out of the forest and through clearings frequently. I follow the animals or try to anticipate where they may be going, trying to catch them in a place where I can see them. The main thing while hunting this country is to remain patient.

David Brooks
Copalis, Washington

• • •

Walk old roads or game trails slowly and quietly, listening for animals crunching around in the brush. (They can't move quietly through it, either.) Once you locate a herd, sneak in as close as you can on the trail and wait for them to come to you. If you head into the brush after them, your chances of getting a shot are slim. Keep the wind in your favor, use the trail as your shooting lane, and be patient. You'll be surprised how many times elk will step into view if you give them time.

Tony Pettis
Newport, Oregon

• • •

Study topo maps and talk to local foresters (federal, state, and private) to locate clear-cuts, old skid trails, and natural meadows. Scout these locations for sign, and when you hunt them be in position and ready at first light. When all else fails, try kneepads and a .44 magnum.

Fred Benton
Mount Shasta, California

• • •

I hunt the southwest Washington coastal range, scouting from June on, looking for the deepest, nastiest hole around. I prefer a marsh with feed, cover, water, and escape routes. Many people hunt too large an area. Keep it small, as elk are very habitual animals. Narrow it down as elk season approaches. If you do, the odds swing in your favor. Think wily whitetail.

Bill Mahitka
Skamokawa, Washington

• • •

The bush here on the Sunshine Coast of British Columbia can get as thick as—well, it's pretty thick. The elk feed along logging roads at night, also in logging slash piles and small clearings, on salmonberry bushes, elderberry, sword ferns, and salal. During the day they bed in thickets, heavy timber, and alder bottoms. Elk tend to only stay in an area for a few days, then move a few miles.

When I find an area that is traveled quite heavily, I will check it out every couple of days, always approaching with the breeze in my face. Locate a good area, and either still-hunt or set up a tree-stand. Be patient. You can hear them and smell them coming.

Bill Ellis
Sechelt, British Columbia

• • •

Presented with thick undergrowth, I would try scouting for active game trails and try to find areas along these trails where you could set up ground blinds or, if circumstances allow, get a tree stand or some sort of platform to get a higher vantage point to be able to look and watch from above instead of trying to see through the branches. Good luck and shoot straight.

Tim Barrett
Rifle, Colorado

• • •

I typically look for open, sedge-dominated wet-land areas or river bottoms adjacent to dense conifer stands, and set up on the down-wind side during early morning and late-afternoon hours to watch for elk. The herbaceous vegetation in these wetlands and riparian bottoms will have more moisture than anything else in the landscape in the late summer/early fall, making them preferred elk browsing locations come the fall hunting seasons. Once elk are in your open wetland, use the dark and dense conifer stand to circle in close to them. Another tactic is to walk quiet-surfaced trails that pass by or through small gaps (two acres or less), which occur in even the most heavily timbered landscapes here. Elk will feed in these gaps more frequently during hunting seasons, feeling more secure than in larger clear-cuts or fields. Walk by these gaps carefully in the predawn darkness (keeping wind in your favor, of course!), and listen for the sounds of elk feeding. Once elk are located by sound, wait for the morning sun to come to give you a shot. Cow calls are also very useful in this landscape.

Mark Swanson
Seattle, Washington

QUESTION 4

I'd like to kill a cow elk with my bow. Is there an effective way to call in a cow elk? What tactics would you suggest?

Andy Tkach
Buffalo, Wyoming

• • •

I have called in a cow elk while attempting to bring in a 6x6 herd bull across 200 yards of open meadow. Spotting the herd feeding in the middle of the meadow, I set up in some timber at its edge with the wind in my favor. The bull was not interested in my "lonesome" cow call, but the cows and calves would lift their heads each time I vocalized. Then I tried a "lost calf" call. One young cow immediately ran directly at me and stood broadside at fifteen yards looking for the "lost calf."

In another instance, a friend and I were on a trail when a bull began bugling, grunting, and raking trees. A cow suddenly appeared, coming up the ridge through dark timber. She passed by on our left at about eighty yards. We figured she was the lead cow and the herd would follow. We thought we could speed the bull's arrival by cow- and calf-calling to him. The cow that passed us suddenly turned and ran back to within twenty yards. The wind swirled, and she caught our scent and bolted.

Calf-calling seems to bring out the moth- erly instincts in the cows, urging them to come to the aid of that "lost calf."

Steve Gentile
Colorado Springs, Colorado

• • •

I've been bowhunting elk in Utah for nearly fif- teen years. Most recently I've focused on spike and cow hunting, because crowds can be avoided in areas with few branch-antlered bull permits. I have had positive experiences with a cow call, bringing in bulls that had several cows with them. If you bring in a bull during the rut, he will most likely bring you a cow.

Scott Mervin
Salt Lake City, Utah

• • •

Use a good cover-up scent. Find a continuously used feeding ground and bedding area, and set up a ground blind or treestand with good shooting lanes beside or above the route used between the areas. Stay still until you are sure you aren't being watched. Do "light" or "curious" cow talk, and every few minutes do a mew that sounds like a calf looking for its mother. Cows—even some "nurse cows" with several calves around them—will come in to see what's going on.

Dennis Tandberg
Harlowton, Montana

• • •

Although hunters have really overdone it with the various elk calls on the market, they can still be effective. But it does require one more thing: cow-in-heat scent applied to ground or foliage near your setup.

Cows still have sense during the rut, unlike bulls which have really cloudy judgment. But if the wind carries the cow-in-heat scent to a herd, the lead cow will lose her head with jealousy and come in barking. More often than not, the bull will be behind the angry cow about seventy-five to a hundred yards, raking up saplings and bugling to impress and claim the new-found cow.

Stay thirty yards or so off to one side, so your scent isn't mixed in with the cow-in-heat scent. Use a treestand so the alert cow looking for a fight doesn't see you. A few light cow yelps will drive the lead cow nuts. Be sure not to call more than once every ten minutes, and do it lightly.

Roger P. Ternyak
Lakewood, Colorado

• • •

In some cases cows will come to cow calls; sometimes they will even walk in to a bugle. But if you really want to call cow elk, imitate a calf in distress.

A few years ago I saw video footage of a black bear galloping into a herd of elk, bowling over a young calf, turning around and picking it up by its shoulder blades, and carrying it off under a tree to eat it. The calf kept calling with a short, high-pitched, raspy cry, about one per second. The whole herd of cows came running, but they couldn't drive the bear off.

I have tried this type of calling on cows, and it works great. When you imitate these distressed calf sounds, you cannot get too high a pitch. Predators will come in as fast as any cow, however, so be careful.

Wayne Carlton
Montrose, Colorado

• • •

I suggest hunting the early part of the season, before the bulls round up the cows into harems. There will be fewer eyes, ears, and noses to fool, and it will be easier to take advantage of their curiosity. Carefully move through the timber while softly mewing, preferably with a diaphragm. When you see a cow or when one responds to your calling, set up in front of good cover to block your outline. Be sure to set up where you have several shooting lanes. As an elk moves in to investigate, use your call to maneuver it into position for a broadside or slightly quartering-away shot.

Come to full draw when her head is behind a tree, and hit the call to stop the elk when she's in position for a shot.

Rob Sherman
Cheyenne, Wyoming

QUESTION 5

I have been applying for a special elk permit for years without success, but this year I finally drew one. I'm not very familiar with the area where my permit is good, and I have no idea how or where to hunt it. What do I do now?

John J. Woods
Clinton, Massachusetts

• • •

The first thing you need to do is purchase a Forest Service or other type of map that will show creeks, springs, buttes, points, and other landmarks. Then call the game biologist and/or forester in the area and follow along as they give you tips on where the highest concentrations of elk are.

Next you should purchase 7.5-minute topographic maps, which can be ordered by phone at 1-888-ASK-USGS, or purchase software, such as that offered by National Geographic, which generates topographic maps of areas you specify. With these maps you can study the terrain in detail and learn a lot about your new area before you set foot in it. For example, by studying contour lines in steep terrain you can identify benches where elk might like to bed down. Try to stay centered between roads. Look for places elk may pass through often, such as saddles, meadows, and springs. If you are able to go and scout the area at all, keep an eye out for campsites with high meat poles; most hunters leave those big signs up saying, "Lots of elk hang around here during elk season."

John Hoiseth
Albany, Oregon

• • •

A good start for your long-distance scouting preparation is to call the game and fish wardens or biologists in the area you plan to hunt. While

USGS topographic maps and the popular (at least in the West) *DeLorme Atlas & Gazetteer* will show you the general lay of the land, local wildlife managers can help narrow your search.

As a Montana game warden, I receive quite a few calls from out-of-state hunters looking for a good starting point on their western hunt. It's tough to give any foolproof advice, but I can usually point folks in the right direction as to topography, elevation, and hunting tactics, which change depending on the weather, hunting pressure, and stage of the rut. Rifle season during an early backcountry hunt will be quite a bit different compared to an early-season bowhunt in the foothills.

That said, lots of shoe leather and long hours is the only recipe for success in most cases. If you are finding elk and/or sign in the area you are hunting, stick with it. If you aren't finding fresh sign, don't be afraid to work a new area. Under any kind of hunting pressure, most herds won't hesitate to move a few miles farther into the brush. Walk-in areas behind locked gates usually hold elk long after the easily accessible areas have been picked clean.

Mike Fegely
Superior, Montana

You've heard of "six degrees of separation," haven't you? In theory, no matter where you go, anybody you know or meet knows somebody who knows somebody who knows somebody who knows somebody who also knows you.

Relationships, relationships, relationships can lead to location, location, location when it comes to elk hunting. So start talking to people. Ask them if they know anybody in the state where you plan to hunt. Don't be shy. Make some phone calls, even to complete strangers. They could turn out to be long-lost relatives who happen to own a large western ranch with elk all over it. Or at least fellow RMEF members with some inside information on the very unit where your special permit is good.

Bill Aldrich
Seattle, Washington

Can bull elk pellets be differentiated from those of a cow elk? If so, how?

John Vieira
Palisade, Colorado

• • •

I believe there is a way to differentiate between bull and cow elk pellets. I believe it has to do with taste and texture, but I have yet to find anyone willing to test my theory.

Bruce Bennett
Sturgis, South Dakota

Here in the San Juans we find the cow elk's pellets to be sweeter and more tender.

Al Kvasnak
Durango, Colorado

• • •

Yes, bull elk pellets can be differentiated from cow elk pellets. The bull pellets are shaped more like a watermelon, or rounder, while cow pellets are tapered down on one end, but not by much. Size and color don't mean much; those have to do with season and type of feed.

Dennis Tandberg
Harlowton, Montana

• • •

I think bull elk pellets can be differentiated from those of a cow elk. The bull pellets are larger, tapered to a slight point, thicker in size, and darker. The cow pellets are smaller, lighter in color, and more rounded. But try the taste test: if they are sweet, they have to be from a nice, tender cow.

Edward Rybarczyk
Rosedale, Maryland

I was always taught that bull elk pellets are clumped together due to the higher levels of testosterone. After more research I think this is not always the case. I think the clumping of pellets is more likely a result of irregular activities prior to the bowel movement. This, in turn, could be a result of the rut. Higher levels of testosterone, irregular physical activity, irregular diet, longer or shorter periods of resting, etc., could cause the pellets to clump together. Bulls have more stress factors during the rut than do cows, so I think more times than not, during the rut, clumped pellets will be from a bull.

Lyn Cotter
Gepp, Arkansas

• • •

When elk are consuming rich but moist summer forage, the feces are soft and pellets are not formed. When pellets are formed, those of the old and large male tend to be larger, relatively shorter, with a point at one end and an indentation at the other. The pellets of females tend to be relatively thinner and longer, pointed at both ends and more irregular in size than those of the male.

In the rut the reduction in forage intake by large males leads to smaller pellets, at times misformed. According to ancient European hunter lore, this does not apply to young male red deer. (Elk are a subspecies of red deer.)

Therefore, one might be able to distinguish the pellets of the two sexes only under rather narrow conditions, which means that usually one cannot do it.

Val Geist, wildlife biologist
Port Alberni, British Columbia

What's the best way to support your rifle in the field? Is it a bad idea to use a tree limb to support your rifle when you're shooting?

Christian Bouck
Denver, Colorado

• • •

I hunt in Arizona and New Mexico and cover a lot of ground. I have made a staff out of a yucca stalk that's light but strong, as tall as myself, with a leather thong through it. It helps keep me steady while climbing hills, supports my binoculars when glassing, and provides a firm shooting platform whether standing or kneeling. I grip the staff with my off hand and put the rifle over my forearm. It works great. And you don't have to go find a tree to lean on when you see an animal you want to shoot.

Alan Kowalski
Tucson, Arizona

• • •

I am a very strong believer in always using a rest of any kind, including a tree limb, or leaning against a tree trunk. Bipods, shooting sticks, daypacks or fanny packs, on the ground or over rocks or clumps of sagebrush for sitting or prone shots . . . I will use anything I can to avoid wounding an animal. I will often pass up a chance rather than shoot offhand.

Tony Hoyt
Arlee, Montana

• • •

Using a tree limb is a bad idea if the limb moves, but a good idea if the limb is sturdy enough to stay still while you aim and shoot. If no solid tree limb is available, the prone and sitting positions are good. Shooting sticks or bipods are helpful if you can handle the extra weight and setup time. I don't recommend any offhand shot at game animals.

Dennis Tandberg
Harlowton, Montana

QUESTION **8**

What's the most important thing for a first-time elk hunter to know?

Rodney Cole
Cottage Grove, Wisconsin

• • •

The most important thing is to have all your equipment in top working order. And the most important piece of equipment is your body. Most elk hunts will get you into some combination of high altitude, steep topography, thick brush, bad weather, and long hikes. If your body is not prepared for these conditions, you're less likely to get an opportunity at a big bull or effectively use your other equipment, i.e., your gun or bow.

Garry Jebousek
Salem, Oregon

They say 90 percent of the elk killed are taken by 10 percent of the hunters. I've been successful every year for the past twenty-nine years, and I believe there are four things a first-time elk hunter needs to know.

1. Be in good enough shape to go where the elk are.
2. Understand elk well enough to know where they might be at a given time, day, and season, and why.
3. Know the area you are hunting so you can concentrate on hunting instead of worrying about where the truck is or how to get home.
4. Take the time to do it right. Don't expect to put in a few days spread out over the season and come home with an elk. Sometimes it'll take you a day to find the elk, a day to blow it on your first try at getting close, and a third to figure them out and connect.

Of these four things, I think being in good enough shape to get where the elk are is the most important.

Norm Larson
Wilson, Wyoming

Humility and patience. The first-time elk hunter had better have a lot of both if he or she hopes to make it through the first season. I first patterned elk movement from what I knew about whitetails. I looked for funnels in the terrain and narrow crossovers that offered cover to move between feeding areas and bedding locations. The elk taught me a lot of hard lessons the first year, and every year thereafter. Carry a notepad, make lots of observations, and study them during the off-season. You'll learn more every year.

Eric Paulikonis
Colorado Springs, Colorado

• • •

The most important thing to know can depend on where you hunt. Those of us who hunt in the Southwest, for example, don't have the luxury of cold weather to help protect the meat. If you only have about eight hours to find, clean, field-dress, and get your elk to the butcher before it spoils, you must plan ahead. You don't want to waste 400 pounds of very tasty meat.

Roger Hollister
Glendale, Arizona

Develop a strong mindset to define success in terms of the hunt instead of the kill. Focusing on the adventure will result in few, if any, unsuccessful elk hunts.

Charles Spoon
Huson, Montana

• • •

Many first-time elk hunters have had some experience already with other big game, such as mule deer, white-tailed deer, and antelope. Take what you have learned about these different animals and throw it all out, because elk are different animals altogether. There are many books, magazine articles, and videos on elk hunting, so do your homework and be prepared. Also, choose the right weapon and bullet. I prefer magnum rounds; it is a more humane way to dispatch the animal. Also be prepared to sell the boat and golf clubs because your free time in summer and fall will now belong to elk hunting.

Kelly Worthen
Roy, Utah

• • •

Know your firearm and use it safely. After that, have maps of your hunting area, a GPS, and a compass, and know how to use them. After that, when around experienced elk hunters, keep your mouth shut and your ears open.

Regan Dean
Butte, Montana

• • •

Know your target and what's beyond it. You can't call the bullet back.

David Anderson
Post Falls, Idaho

• • •

Understand the heritage and history of elk hunting. This will take you back to the basics of hunting. Learn the behavior of elk in their natural habitat. Then go and have a fun and safe hunt.

Sam Shelley
Gulf Breeze, Florida

• • •

You don't have to kill (or even see) an elk to have fun. Learn to enjoy and learn from the many moods of elk country, and every hunt will be a success.

Ben Long
Kalispell, Montana

Know what to do with it once it's on the ground. This is not a white-tailed deer. It is a huge animal that takes careful planning long before you pull the trigger or release the arrow. I saw someone shoot an elk in the bottom of a very deep canyon when it was extremely hot in September. It spoiled long before the last piece could be carried to the truck. This is not only irresponsible, it is also illegal. If you are prepared before the hunt, you and your family will enjoy some of the best meat on the planet.

Bill Blunt
Red Bluff, California

• • •

Do some pre-season scouting in the area you plan to hunt. Plan on hiking a lot. This will not only help you locate the elk, but will help get you in shape for the upcoming season. Topo maps and a GPS are great tools for this. Going in prepared will make your elk hunt more enjoyable and, we hope, more successful.

Steve Miller
Stansbury Park, Utah

Know that your hunt can be 100 percent successful without ever pulling the trigger or releasing an arrow. You will be hunting in some of the most pristine landscapes that this world has to offer while chasing the most magnificent animal on earth. Hunt as hard as you possibly can, but think about why you are really there and enjoy every step along the way.

Time spent with fathers, mothers, sons, daughters, and friends is the most important reason for hunting. Every fall I am fortunate enough to spend ten days twenty-eight miles by horseback inside the wilderness of Wyoming with my hunting partner: my dad. Every hunt on which we have gone over the years has been successful, often with both of us shooting a bull, other times where only one of us could harvest a bull, and times when we never fired a shot but came home overflowing with memories. Last year I had a 340-class bull at sixty yards but couldn't get a shot. It was an experience that few people get to endure and I will remember it forever. The highlight, however, was the 6x7 that my dad shot during the last ten minutes of the hunt after a one-and-a-half-hour bugling frenzy between hunters and the elk.

If you hunt hard and enjoy everything along the way, success is guaranteed.

Dave Kleckner
Oregon, Wisconsin

• • •

Patience, persistence, and perseverance come to mind when I think of elk hunting. You want to move slowly into the wind, into some of the thickest, steepest timber you can find. Stay with it regardless of the weather. Hunt all day, every day, until the final minute of the hunt. You'll have time to relax and recuperate after your elk is in the freezer.

Mark Sullivan
Poland, Ohio

• • •

Try not to be stupid. The list of stupid things that could be done on an elk hunt is endless. Prepare yourself by researching as much as you can about hunting ethics, safety, how your fellow hunters will react when you tell them you shot an elk at the bottom of a ravine, and what the early signs of cardiac arrhythmia are as you haul your elk out of the bottom of the ravine by yourself.

Only under certain circumstances should you let on that this is your first elk hunt. If you're going to be hunting with fellows who have not had a lot of success and you bag an elk on opening morning, your efforts will be written off as beginner's luck.

If you'll be hunting with people who get their elk year after year because they have a secret honey hole where the elk are big and so old they no longer care if a hunter is around, then my best advice to you is to bring me along. I will personally make sure that you don't do anything stupid.

Mike Cox
Estes Park, Colorado

• • •

Moving too fast and too much is the most common error for first-time elk hunters. Once fresh sign is found, advance only a few steps at a time, then stop and carefully look all around. Move forward again only after being convinced no elk is in sight.

John Vieira
Palisade, Colorado

• • •

Carry in your daypack everything you'd need to spend the night. Tell someone where you are going. Don't ever think you'll always be able to make it back to camp or your vehicle before bad weather sets in. An elk is not worth your life.

Scott Davis
Phoenix, Oregon

• • •

Know what to do if your first hunt is successful. An elk might weigh as much as four white-tailed bucks. Quartering the bull is the most common method of butchering him into transportable parts. Some hunters bone all the meat out in the field to reduce weight, and I have done this before, but now I always haul the extra weight because less meat is exposed to the air, dirt, flies, and hair that way.

Take along four meat bags, one for each quarter. A hunting buddy of mine turned me on to king-sized pillowcases, and they work great to protect the meat. I hunt with a pack frame on (the Dwight Schuh pack is a great one) so I can get the backstraps, tenderloins, and a quarter out on my first trip. Bring a few sharp knives in your pack so you don't have to waste time sharpening while you could be skinning and quartering. Have a plan for the meat once back in camp, too.

It's critical to keep it cool. We pack huge coolers and get the meat on bagged ice once we've hung it in the shade for a day or two. Some dry ice in the coolers makes regular ice last longer. Elk meat is fabulous, and planning for a successful hunt will ensure that your hard-earned meat gets back home in the best condition possible.

Justin Karnopp
Missoula, Montana

• • •

The first thing is to purchase a very good pair of binoculars. Learn to use them to look deeper into trees, grass, bushes, shadows, long distances, etc. Do not look for the full body of an animal, just parts. Learn the different color of parts on an elk, and be thinking of those colors. Do not think or look for deer, or you will overlook elk. Do lots of scouting if possible. Act like you are hunting while you are scouting; it's good practice. Look for elk where they eat, sleep, hide, and travel, not where you want them to be, such as beside a road (on the uphill side), in open areas with easy access, or by camp.

Dennis Tandberg
Harlowton, Montana

When you go on your first elk hunt, hunt with someone familiar with processing meat in the field. Two books, *Elk Hunting* by Jim Zumbo, and *Elk Talk* by Don Laubach and Mark Henckel, both deal with the subject. However, the best materials I've seen on the subject appear in the Elk Foundation's *Bugle* magazine in the form of letters and articles from other hunters. A little careful planning can help your first elk hunting experience become a fond memory instead of a huge and unpleasant "learn by your mistakes" session.

John Wallace
Vancouver, Washington

• • •

Learn a bit about elk behavior. Learn some basic spotting and tracking skills. Learn to look at the little details around you. In short, learn to immerse yourself in the elk's world for a time. That way, you'll always get something out of the hunt even if you don't see an elk.

Bob Cherry
Idaho Falls, Idaho

That's easy: Buy a straitjacket and some Valium. You'll need them at least once during your first few seasons (your first week if using a bow).

Bruce Morrison

Altadena, California

The past three years I have drawn some coveted archery tags, but I keep getting saddled with the early hunt and it is pre-rut. There is no bugling, it is always hot, and I have trouble locating bulls. Can anyone help me solve this problem?

Michael Carter
Los Lunas, New Mexico

• • •

The best way to locate bulls in the pre-rut is to find a water hole that elk have been using frequently, then set up a treestand at the yardage you feel comfortable shooting. You should see plenty of bulls.

Riker Jacobson
Irwin, Idaho

• • •

One solution would be to get to know where wallows are located in your area. This scouting can be done from mid-summer until the snow flies. This is a great way to become intimately acquainted with elk country and brings pleasure in and of itself. An easier course is to find a good overlook at elevation, and sit quietly without silhouetting yourself. Glass and glass some more.

John Vieira
Palisade, Colorado

• • •

The bulls are not in rut, but they are thinking about it. They are not far from the cows. Find the cows; then go up on top of the small mountains in the area. Most of the mountains around here are volcanic and have a bowl on top. It is cooler up there, and a lot of them hold some water. The steeper the better, but you have to be there first. It is very easy to push them off these small mountaintops.

Roger A. Hollister
Glendale, Arizona

• • •

Hunt pre-bugling bulls using the same tactics as in the rut, except do mostly (95 percent) cow and calf talk—just enough to get their attention and curiosity. Use a good cover-up scent and good binoculars. Scout the area, being careful not to disturb the elk as they will change areas more easily.

Work close to a water source, if possible, but stay out of sight. Whatever the case, do your homework and be patient.

Dennis Tandberg
Harlowton, Montana

What pre-hunt preparations should one or two hunters make if they won't have an ATV or horses to pack out the meat?

Bob Cherry
Idaho Falls, Idaho

• • •

Pre-hunt preparations for packing out that bull that is six miles from camp are all about physical and mental conditioning. For some hunters, a complete physical exam is a must. Any regular exercise regime will help.

Mental conditioning is all about anticipating problems. The cart you were going to use to get the meat out—do you have a tire repair kit?

Make sure all equipment is in good working condition. You don't need the hassle of something not working when you need it most. And take care of things requiring attention at home or work before you go. Once you're out there, who needs the distraction?

Be familiar with the area you are hunting. Is there an easier route to pack the meat out? Are you prepared to care for the meat if you can't get it out right away?

Don't get frustrated or stressed about things. Enjoy where you are. And be sure to let a couple of people know where you are in case the unimaginable happens.

Being physically and mentally prepared demands extra attention. The cost is too high to let anything slide.

Grant Bowie
*Dawson Creek, British
Columbia*

• • •

If you anticipate personally packing out your meat, use this formula: Think, think, and work.

1. Think about how you plan to field-dress your elk. Quartered, boned, caped? Think

about how meat, head, and hide will be packaged for transport. Think about the equipment required for field-dressing and packaging. Think about the distance you might need to cover and the number of trips it would take.

2. Think about scenarios likely to come into play: weather impacts, overnight storage of meat, bear visits, etc. Have a plan for scenarios, and adjust your equipment inventory to match.

3. Work—as in work out. You are facing several trips with heavy pack loads. My experience has been with backpack trips across difficult terrain (as in long and steep) in remote areas. If you are in good condition and follow the think-think-work formula, you will get much enjoyment out of this phase of the hunt.

Bill Fore
Dallas, Texas

• • •

I would suggest being in excellent physical condition. Improve endurance by hiking as much as you can this summer. In the weight room, concentrate on your legs and back. These muscle groups do most of the work when packing out an animal.

Two things you can buy will greatly ease your work. First, get a game cart. Most are made for either one- or two-person operation and hold half an elk. Game carts don't work well in snow, so if there's a chance of running into some of the white stuff, toss a couple of sturdy sleds into your truck. The big, high-sided ice fishing sleds work best, but normal, plastic trough-style sleds will do. You can easily put half an elk onto a big sled.

These contraptions hold more meat than a pack frame, but that doesn't mean it's going to be easy. It's imperative that you are in good enough shape to handle the chore.

Brad Nielsen
Florence, Montana

• • •

I believe there are at least four pre-hunt preparations to consider. The first is to get familiar with the area you will hunt, by map study, on-site scouting, and talking with area residents, hunters, and game and forestry officials in the area. The second is to become physically fit to pack out heavy loads. The third is learning how to cut up or bone out an animal. The fourth is gathering the proper equipment, including a good pack-board, knife sharpener, GPS unit, compass, and surveyor's flagging to locate the kill site.

Jack Gaudette
Port Orchard, Washington

• • •

First, find a hunting partner with a size eighteen neck and a size two hat. (Just kidding!) You need to know how to skin and bone out your downed elk so you're not packing out all that heavy bone. There are books and videos out there to help you understand the process. Removing the bones (or removing the meat off the bones) also helps the meat to cool quicker. You also need to get a good backpack, quality meat bags, and hopefully a bone saw to remove those antlers.

Harley Metz
Grand Junction, Colorado

• • •

The most important item for pre-hunt preparation is to gather knowledge. You must know what to do after the elk is down. I skin the elk on one side and debone that side, then roll the elk over and repeat. The next most important item is physical conditioning. You must be reasonably able to pack seventy or eighty pounds to the nearest road. (Or make more trips with less weight.) Third, you need to gather a few essentials. My checklist includes two knives, sharpening steel, cotton meat bags, twenty feet of nylon cord, small saw, several pairs of medical gloves, and an external pack frame.

Carroll Hanft
Addison, Pennsylvania

• • •

Know your personal limitations. Obtain the most recent contour map of the area. Identify all roads, and check with landowners and appropriate agencies to be sure the roads are still open. Avoid hunting down in deep, steep canyons with no access from below. No matter how fit you are, there is a limit as to how far you can pack out the meat before it spoils. And elk don't always die where you would like them to, even with the best of personal discipline and judgment. Consider identifying in advance someone with horses and mules whom you can call to pack out the meat before it spoils.

Richard E. Nelson
Bend, Oregon

• • •

Know the terrain, and know your limits. Before you shoot, you must be sure you can physically overcome the geography to recover the animal from the place where it may fall. If you have any doubts about your ability to get the meat out before it spoils, don't shoot!

Kevin J. Burdick
Auburn, California

• • •

See your physician to make sure you do not have underlying cardiovascular problems. Then exercise. Start walking, hiking, or running a minimum of three days a week for at least three miles or thirty minutes per session. Weightlifting exercises such as squats, deadlifts, power-cleans, and bench presses will strengthen the large muscle groups necessary to pack out an elk. These should also be done at least three times per week with a rest day between sessions. This doesn't sound as sexy as buying a new short magnum or the latest camo, but I guarantee that the guy in shape, wearing an old red plaid jacket and carrying an ancient .30-06, will bring home more elk than the out-of-shape hunter equipped with the latest fashion camo and whiz-bang rifle.

Be ready to butcher and quarter your animal on the spot. I utilize a method commonly called "Indian quartering." After your animal is down, you do not gut it. Instead, you skin the animal and remove the meat from the carcass, leaving the viscera and most of the bones behind. First you peel off the hide from one entire side, folding it down on the ground like a tarp. Next, remove the front quarter by cutting under the shoulder blade and disarticulating it from the chest. Then remove the hind quarter by disarticulating the femur at the pelvic joint. Now strip off the backstrap by cutting close to the spine and peeling off all that prime meat. Next, strip off the rib meat and bone out the neck. Lastly, reach into the abdominal cavity just forward of the pelvis and carefully remove the tenderloin. Flip carcass over and repeat.

I carry six game bags (the small, light-weight, roll-up variety like those made by Alaska

Game Bags): quarters, with bones left in or removed, go into four of the game bags. Backstraps and tenderloins go into another bag; rib meat, neck meat, and other trimmings go into the last bag. Go to the Alaska Department of Fish and Game, and order their "Field Care of Big Game" video.

Get a good pack frame that's padded, ergonomically designed, and adjustable to fit your body. Practice hiking with this fully loaded. Now go out and bring one back for the freezer.

Ronald LeBeaumont,
M.D. *Cheyenne, Wyoming*

• • •

I have packed out eight elk in the last seven seasons with only a pair of hiking boots and a backpack. Obviously being in top physical condition is a must. So is choosing an area from which you know you are capable of packing out your meat.

My gear list includes two knives, a bone saw, mesh game bags, rope to secure and hang quarters, contractor-grade (three-mil) trash bags, and a quality backpack. I have found that a sturdy internal-frame pack is the most comfortable way to carry heavy loads. I place a heavy-duty trash bag in my pack, fill the bag with pre-cooled cuts of meat, then transfer the meat into a marine-sized cooler when I reach the vehicle.

It's not a bad idea to carry some pepper spray when hauling meat, because elk country is bear country, and bears like meat, too.

Kevin E. Wagner
Highlands Ranch, Colorado

• • •

Even with an ATV or horses you can't always get right to your animal. To cool the meat quickly and get rid of extra weight, learn to bone out your animal. Obtain a good backpack and large canvas meat bags, good skinning and boning knives, and sharpener. You will find, with some practice, that this is a simple process, and be amazed at how quickly and cleanly you can get all the meat off a carcass.

Dave Kruse
Milton-Freewater, Oregon

• • •

Buy a good heavy-duty pack frame that fits you well. Then adjust it for your build and load it with something heavy and awkward and go for a hike. You could buy one of the heavy-duty wheeled carts on the market, but some wilderness areas will not allow them so be sure to check that out before spending money for one. Also if the area you are going to hunt is heavily forested or rocky and steep, they aren't much good either.

One item I take along is one of those cheap plastic toboggans. If there is snow, you can slide a lot of weight on one of these. One more thing you can do: when you get to your hunt area, visit the horse camps in the area and see if you can arrange to have someone pack an elk out for you.

John Cannon
Lusk, Wyoming

How can you hunt bulls when they stay up all night rutting and feeding and quit talking by 8 a.m.?

Floyd Cox
Joplin, Missouri

• • •

A great way to hunt these bulls in the morning is to have them located by sunset the day before. Usually the bulls are at their destination for the night no later than one hour after dark. The key is to arrive in the morning before light and set up along their path to where they will be heading once it starts to get light.

It really helps to get up extra early, because you don't want to rush yourself or waste your time trying to catch up to the elk if you arrive after they've passed.

Adam Moro
Pinetop, Arizona

• • •

Consider taking a leisurely midnight stroll. Tread softly, pausing often to listen for elk talk, bull or cow. Approach only as close as necessary to determine the approximate location of the source of the siren song. Then return directly to camp rather than spreading your scent by dallying.

Using maps and/or personal knowledge of the terrain, select a point with a commanding view of the area where the elk were last heard. If a funnel between the elk's breakfast nook and bed is within range, so much the better. Be there at daybreak.

Whether your ambush bears fruit or not, the heightened senses of sound and smell in a nighttime scouting adventure are rewards in themselves. You will never forget your midnight scouting experience.

John Vieira
Palisade, Colorado

In mountainous country, elk generally move down at night and up in the morning. The best way to find these bulls is to be listening at least thirty minutes before they stop bugling. Keep track of the amount of time between each call, and try to be quiet and listening at the right time for locating the elk each time they bugle. Mark each call either on a map or in your head. Then get well above the line of calls.

Give yourself enough time to get above them and set up. Remember the patterns of the thermal currents, and keep the wind in your favor while trying your best to get ready within 300 yards. Then create a series of high-pitched, squeaky, young bull bugles. (Generally, make four to six of these in one minute.) This sends either of two messages to any big bull in the vicinity: A young bull is really excited about a hot cow in the area, and/or that young bull is in the big bull's territory. Either way, that big bull is going to want to push him out.

If the elk have already bedded, you might get a low, guttural, half-hearted bugle from the herd bull that makes it sound like he is drowning. This usually means that he won't move for a couple of hours unless he's hot for a cow or ticked off. The only way to hunt a bull like that is to get close and throw a few challenging bugles at him. Don't overdo it, though. If he's not in the mood you might run him off.

Chad A. White
Missoula, Montana

• • •

Rutting bulls do not carry watches. When the rut is on, it is on—without regard for time or temperature. I've bugled and shot bulls at ninety-five degrees Fahrenheit at high noon in Arizona, and in an ice storm at dawn in Montana. I've also quietly moved in on bugling elk in the middle of the night, when several satellite bulls were pestering the herd bull. Elk don't seem to move far in the night, but a herd bull will try to haze his cows away from the circling satellite bulls. So determine the general direction of the movement of the herd, and keep edging in closer without bugling or cow calling.

If you feel you are very close to the herd by dawn, try some light cow-calling to imitate a cow that the herd bull might have lost track of. He'll try to beat a satellite bull to the misplaced cow. Don't overdo the calling. Be patient, and keep easing along with the general movement of the herd. You should have action from either the satellite bulls or the herd bull before the sun "burns" you.

Bill Sansom
St. Regis, Montana

• • •

The more moonlight, the more time they're active at night, and the earlier they go to bed in the thick brush for the day. So if you get some real dark nights, from heavy clouds and/or the dark of the moon, the better your chance of finding them still up and about at daybreak or dusk.

Steve Hopkins
Tucson, Arizona

If I had to spend a night in the woods, what would you say are the most important things to have with me to make sure I survive?

Chris Hyland
Walla Walla, Washington

• • •

Basic knowledge of survival skills is the best "insurance policy" you can give yourself. The most important survival skill is proper shelter construction. Staying alive in very cold conditions requires dead air space, which can be accomplished by stuffing a shelter with forest debris such as leaves. Hydration is second. Dehydration, especially at high altitudes, can cause internal damage after twenty-four hours without water. Fire-making is third. Carry matches or a lighter and some form of sure-to-burn firestarter. Food is last; you can go sixty days without it. Be prepared to provide yourself with shelter, water, fire, and food—in that order—and your overnight stay could be not only survivable but enjoyable.

Rick Rhoads
Bernville, Pennsylvania

• • •

1. Keep your head. If you lose that, you're likely to just get more lost, and possibly hurt yourself wandering around in the dark.
2. Make sure you have matches or a lighter, along with some toilet paper for firestarter. Fire is your friend. It's amazing how, no matter where you are, if you're able to strike up a fire, it's "home" for now.
3. A sharp hatchet or knife is important. A good blade will help you gather material

to build a shelter. An emergency blanket helps, too.

Butch Grusing
Fountain, Colorado

• • •

Take along a lightweight, waterproof six-foot by eight-foot tarp and at least twenty-five feet of light rope to construct a lean-to. Set it up fifty feet or so above the bottom of any drainage: cold air sinks, and a slightly elevated camp can be ten to fifteen degrees warmer at night.

Carry waterproof matches and/or a butane lighter, plus Vaseline-soaked cotton balls which make great firestarter in almost any weather. Build your fire just outside your lean-to, with a wall of rock against the outer side of the fire to reflect heat back at you.

If you're in Colorado, buy a hunting and fishing license even if you are just planning a day hike. The price of the license includes a twenty-five-cent surcharge for Search and Rescue (S&R). It's cheap insurance in case S&R has to go looking for you. Last year I took a bad spill from a horse and had to be flown out by helicopter. The bill came to $14,000, which was covered completely by the S&R surcharge.

Jay Houston
Colorado Springs, Colorado

• • •

Water is essential, perhaps a pint in a cool environment; more in a hot one. Food is not immediately vital, and most of us Americans carry a Happy Meal or ten stored in our torsos.

A dry layer of clothing—either wool or synthetic, never cotton—next to the skin can be critical. Wet clothing transports heat away from the body twenty-five times faster than dry clothing. Keep a spare, dry top, pants or long johns, socks, gloves, and hat with you in case you get wet from exertion, rain, or a slip into the creek. Wet clothes can spell death, or at best a miserable night. Off with the wet, on with the dry. Add a hooded windbreaker to your survival clothes kit.

A cigarette lighter is far more reliable and wind-resistant than the traditional alternative. But it might not hurt to have some dry "farmer matches" as backup.

Carry a paperback book, preferably one by Pat McManus. Seriously. We tell our kids to "hug a tree" if they become lost. The book works the same way for us grownups. Sit down, calm yourself, catch your breath, and assess your situation. You are okay. The challenge now is to stay okay. Read a few pages and chuckle a bit. Then use the just-read pages to start a warming and spirit-lifting fire.

Allan Reishus, M.D.
Craig, Colorado

• • •

This hunter believes the most important thing to have is confidence. With confidence, an unintended overnight in the woods may even border on being pleasant. Without it, errors of judgment are much more likely. Confidence is easily acquired. It is based on experience. To gain experience, practice staying out overnight with minimal gear. Practice starting a fire. Make it a practice to carry a survival kit, and practice using the contents. As a bonus, building confidence makes for a more enjoyable hunting experience overall. Take care, and have a great hunt.

John Vieira
Palisade, Colorado

First, keep a cool head. Don't panic. Admit you
have to stay out, and deal with it. Find some
shelter from the weather, for example a big tree
with lots of branches. Gather boughs and prop
them up against a tree, log, cliff, or bank so you
can crawl under them. Always carry some type
of firestarter. Be sure to gather lots of wood for
fuel before you settle in. A space blanket is real
handy and does not take up a lot of room in the
daypack.

Water is more critical than food, but something rich and tasty, such as trail mix or power
bars, will not only provide energy but also comfort you and help you stay calm.

Dennis Tandberg
Harlowton, Montana

• • •

Carry a big plastic garbage bag. Climbing into
one of those will help keep you warm and dry.
Hypothermia will be your biggest threat to survival
for an unexpected overnighter. Being wet with the
wind blowing, even in relatively mild temps of
forty to fifty degrees, is a setup for dropping core
body temps and development of hypothermia—a
potential life threatening situation.

The best bet for all sportsmen is to develop and carry a pack to take with you whenever you leave the house to head for the hills. It should contain at least a couple of methods to start a fire, a whistle for signaling help, a flashlight and extra batteries, a map of the area, a compass, a basic first aid kit (to include a couple of days of prescription medications), a knife or better yet a survival tool like a Leatherman, and a big plastic bag or two. A space blanket would also suffice. I carry both.

Keep the pack small enough that you will grab it and carry it with you as routinely as putting your hat on. Most often folks get in the outside overnight scenarios when they least expect it.

Rich Gerhard
Coeur d'Alene, Idaho

QUESTION 13

What's the best tool for field-dressing an elk or other big game animal? I've heard of a guy quartering an elk with a Leatherman, and I imagine if you bone out your meat it can be done with just a knife. But what if you want to take out the rack? You need a saw or hatchet, don't you?

Rich Gerhard
Coeur d'Alene, Idaho

• • •

During the last thirteen years, I have tried many types of knives and saws to dress and quarter elk. I now have what I consider the three best tools.

They are lightweight and durable. First is the Buck cross-lock knife. On one flip-out blade is the best gut hook I have ever found, and on the other side is a great skinning blade. The second tool is made by Stanley products and can be bought at any hardware store. It has a black plastic handle and comes with a replaceable, sawzall-type blade. A compartment in the handle stores a spare blade. The third tool is a folding, pocket-size diamond sharpening tool. Start with a sharp knife, and use the fine-grade diamond sharpening blade to touch up your knife's edge as you work. One more thing I recommend is a good pair of rubber gloves. These are quite flexible and have a great texture that really helps when the work gets slippery with blood.

Dale A. Swiss
Tucson, Arizona

• • •

I highly recommend a five-inch serrated hunting knife by Cutco: their Model 1769C. Last year I shot a nice 5x5 bull in a canyon in Colorado, and needed to quarter and pack it out. I was able to quarter and filet the entire elk with just the one knife without any need to sharpen it. As for taking out the rack, it's not necessary to have a saw or hatchet. A stout knife and a little bit of twisting will separate the base of the skull and the first vertebra. Once you get back to camp, or better yet to the taxidermist, the antlers and skull plate can be removed with a proper bone saw.

By the way, I wouldn't go into the woods without a Leatherman-type tool. While it's not my first choice for quartering an elk, the blade on my model works great for caping in the field, especially around the antler bases. And don't forget a pair of those "full-length" rubber field dressing gloves.

Greg Julian
Maple City, Michigan

• • •

All you need to field-dress a big game animal is a sharp object. My preference is a four- to five-inch straight blade (as opposed to a skinning knife). But I am extremely weight conscious, so I only carry a two-inch Schrade Old Timer. I used that knife to gut and skin an entire elk in Colorado this year. Needless to say, it was pretty dull by the time I got to the skinning part, but it still did the trick. I also carry a small, lightweight

Gerber saw for cutting through the pelvis and cutting the head off in the woods, though you could cut through the hide and neck meat at the base of the skull and twist the head off without any need for a saw.

David Clumpner
Anacortes, Washington

• • •

You could get by with a Leatherman (or other brand of multi-purpose tool), but I think it's worth it to carry a little more weight. I carry two knives, one a folding knife with a serrated blade to cut anywhere that I'll run into hair or bone; these areas dull a regular blade quickly. My other knife is a fixed blade. I also carry a folding saw. I can cut down a carcass to backpacking-sized pieces with it and also cut antlers from the skull.

My son-in-law put me on to carrying a cordless reciprocal saw. This really takes the work out of butchering an elk if you're leaving the bone in. It's worth having in a backpack for the first trip. We leave it on an ATV or in camp until we shoot something.

Dennis Tandberg
Harlowton, Montana

There is a joint right at the base of the skull that you can get through easily with a knife. The whole head is a lot heavier than just antlers and skullplate, but it's a solution if you aren't carrying a saw. I am a butcher and have also done some guiding. I have taken care of many elk with just a knife.

Galen Kalander
Everson, Washington

• • •

I have found that a three-piece combo set with a caper, skinner, and saw is perfect for field dressing an elk . Mine is all in one sheath so it is not bulky or heavy. The two blades are enough knife to skin and quarter (or more), and the saw, while small, cuts the biggest bones.

Alan Kowalski
Tucson, Arizona

In many articles on hunting, the authors talk about walking miles before sunrise to get to their hunting territory. How do they see where they are going? What kind of light source do they use? I'd appreciate any tips about hiking to a hunting spot in the dark.

Dave Schmillen
Longmont, Colorado

• • •

I use a headlamp and a GPS. I like to go to the spot during daylight hours and mark it on my

GPS. Then when I return during the night, I can use the GPS as a guide. I also use a red- or green-filtered headlamp so it doesn't ruin my night vision. Believe it or not, on a clear night you can see a lot without any kind of artificial light source.

Travis Legler
Dewey, Arizona

• • •

In daylight, familiarize yourself with trailside landmarks or make some of your own, so you can reassure yourself you're on the right path. The blackness is not a place or time for exploring or wondering if you're on the right trail. I like headlamps in the LED style. Lots of battery life and a pleasant glow, and they're even nicer with a red lens cover. Wear a brimmed hat, and keep your head slightly down. This will work like cat whiskers, keeping brush from slapping your face or, worse, scratching your eyes. Make sure the wind will be favorable for your walk in the dark. Early-morning thermals tend to flow downhill.

Richard Mitchell
Moscow, Idaho

The best way to hike in the dark is to use a headlamp. Just remember that a light moving around in the dark is something elk are not used to, so when you get close to your hunting area, turn off the light and take a break until you can see well enough to continue without it.

Ryan Johnson
Gunnison, Colorado

• • •

Except on the darkest nights or in the thickest timber, there is usually enough ambient light to get where you want to go without artificial light. Our night vision is better than you think, if you practice a bit. Before you leave your truck, give your eyes a few minutes to adjust to the darkness. Switching a white light on and off effectively destroys your natural night vision, so keep your light in a pocket until you really need it. Chances are you won't.

Steve Fillerup
Elk Ridge, Utah

• • •

The only reason I hike before daylight is if I've put the elk to bed the night before, typically by glassing from a distance. Why hike for miles in the dark to get to a spot that might not have elk? Ordinarily I start hiking at first light; who knows where you might spot elk? Heading into new or unfamiliar country in the dark, even with a map and light source, is a recipe for disaster unless you at least have a trail to follow.

Mike Jenkins
Townsend, Montana

• • •

For over twenty-five years I've been hiking in the dark at least an hour, sometimes three, to get to my deer- and elk-hunting spots. It's important to scout your route in the daylight before you hike in the dark. I use a small flashlight and make sure the batteries are strong, and always carry extra batteries in my pack. Carrying a bigger, stronger light has the advantage of making it easier to find blood and/or wounded game once darkness sets in. You can use your hands or fingers to cover the lens and control the amount of light you're putting out.

Other hunters may be in your area, and some may be scared and careless enough to shoot at a noise or shape moving through the country.

So I leave my light on until it's light enough to discern shapes and movement.

Kevin Joseph
Dolores, Colorado

• • •

I have hunted elk for ten years in Colorado with Crazy Horse Outfitters and Guides. The father-and-son guides, with over 100 years of hunting experience between them, rarely use a flashlight. Any artificial light anywhere around elk is not going to help the hunt. My suggestion is to access your hunting spot by horseback. Horses, especially those trained specifically for elk hunting, can see unbelievably well in the dark and have a keen sense of where they are relative to camp. To me, an elk hunt is not an elk hunt unless it's on horseback. So lose the lights, ditch the backpacks, and get a horse.

Don Cummings
Seymour, Indiana

• • •

Have a partner and go slowly for safety. If you don't feel comfortable or confident, wait until daylight. You might miss your best chance of catching them out in the open, but lots of people still kill elk in the middle of the day. In our area we have lots of game trails that we use to get where the elk are early, or get back to camp after dark. You learn those trails when you scout an area to find out where the elk are. Flagging helps, but be sure to pull it down when you are done.

Dennis Tandberg
Harlowton, Montana

• • •

In my experience, 90 percent of the elk taken are found in 10 percent of the available habitat, and that habitat is usually at least a one-hour hike from the nearest road. If you are to hunt from the break of day until dark, you have to be comfortable in your ability to do the hike in the dark. The first thing to do to become comfortable is to hike the country during the day, before the season opens. Find the best route to these honey holes. One of my favorite passions in the off season is to "rearrange the vegetation" so that you can get from point A to point B in the easiest manner. Use existing landmarks to find your way— a unique stump, pile of rocks, or create your own signs. I like to arrange fallen debris on the down hill side of the trail I want to follow. If you take the time to hike to your spot a few times during the day and pay attention to the details along the way, it will make it much easier in the dark. Avoid using flagging tapes and other commercial markers. They are unsightly garbage to most hunters and other forest users, as well as leading other folks to your favorite spot.

I use a mini-mag flashlight. It is easy to carry (in fact, I carry two and the extra batteries don't take up much room in your pack), it provides more than enough light, and you can get a headband that the flashlight slips into for a handy headlamp when dressing game in the dark. Be sure to take a compass and get the gist of which direction you should be traveling, in case you come to a confusing impasse. As always, take basic survival gear. Going in before daybreak or coming out after dark isn't so scary. Just be prepared!

Richard Gerhard
Coeur d'Alene, Idaho

• • •

First, don't try to hike by night a route you have not hiked in the daytime. You should have picked the spot you intend to hunt at shooting light by its proximity to the food, water source or shelter of the game you seek, or proximity to a travel route between these habitat keys. Verify in the daytime that what you are looking for is there, then hike along the route you intend to take. There are too many possibilities of uncrossable obstacles to attempt a first pass in the dark.

Second, use available natural light. The moon is frequently up and provides enough natural light to pass on good trails and cross meadows and open areas.

Third, rely on your flashlight if you are at all uneasy about your footing. I currently use an LED flashlight with a quick push-button switch tied to my wrist with a loop of stout cord. To avoid side glare which might spook game, I cup the light in my hand so that a thin beam shines directly where I want to look.

Fourth, carry a backup flashlight and spare batteries so you are mentally comfortable and willing to use the light extensively to work it out should you get disoriented.

Tom Harris
Mission, Kansas

What really takes the guesswork out of finding landmarks in the dark is a GPS. One of my first out-of-state elk hunts left me and three of my buddies following a blood trail in the dark, with no GPS. Even though we'd marked our trail with surveyor tape, we still wandered around in circles for hours trying to find our way back to our vehicle. Finally we stopped arguing, prayed and, navigating by the North Star, came out on the road twenty feet from the truck. Using a GPS would have eliminated the guesswork.

Lance Rea
Touchet, Washington

• • •

Walking or hiking to a destination hours before sunrise can be accomplished easily with the right tools. The first tool is a handheld Global Positioning Satellite (GPS). This allows you to see exactly where your destination is, how fast you are traveling, time of day, etc. Most handheld GPSs have computer software that allows the user to pre-load maps so you can see the topography of the area. With or without a GPS unit, always carry a compass and a map of the area. If possible, familiarize yourself with the area during the daylight hours.

The second tool is a headlamp. It keeps your hands free and comes in a wide variety of brands, shapes, and sizes, but the focus should be on compactness and illumination. Even the smallest illuminate a large area that makes it easy for hiking. The batteries also last much longer in an LED headlamp. Some LED headlamps come with a red cover that allows the headlamp to emit red light. This is an old military trick to retain your night vision, and it works surprisingly well.

Safety is the number one concern. It is much more dangerous to hike in low visibility hours. You never want to be rushed when hiking, especially in the dark, because the more you hurry, the greater the chance of a misstep. Allow extra time to arrive at your hunting location.

Ryan Fosness
Rapid City, South Dakota

Is there an effective rule of thumb to determine when elk will come to water to drink?

Tom Sweet
Buford, Georgia

• • •

Elk are big animals; thus they need a lot of water. They are also cud-chewers and need water to chew their cuds. Early in the morning, after they have finished eating, elk will drink before heading to their bedding area to rest and chew their cud. Find a water source the elk are using and set up a blind or stand somewhere along the trail.

During the hours they are in their bedding area (roughly 8 or 9 a.m. until 5 or 6 p.m.), elk will get up and move around from time to time and do a little grazing or browsing. Frequently, between roughly 11 a.m. and 1:30 p.m., the bulls will go check their wallows and drink. Find a wallow that is being used, set up with the wind in your favor, and wait.

Jim Hawkins
Coeur d'Alene, Idaho

• • •

Elk usually water late in the evening, throughout the night, and early in the morning. But there is no way of knowing for sure when or where an elk will go to get a drink of water. In central Montana, where I live, there is water available at many locations, even in a drought.

Scout the water sources in your area and learn which ones are used frequently. Don't spend too much time in the area, though. Your human scent could make the elk change water sources.

Dennis Tandberg
Harlowton, Montana

When do elk go to water? Whenever they get thirsty. They are most likely to go to water early in the morning and late in the afternoon. But I once saw a group of spike bulls watering at a hidden spring at midday. Know where water is available in your area, and pay special attention to water holes that are concealed, not out in the open.

David W. Stewart
East Helena, Montana

Do elk perceive the sounds of an ATV as benign? Do they learn to associate them with danger? Is there a point at which an ATV becomes a liability rather than an asset in elk hunting?

Allen Paprocki
Twin Falls, Idaho

• • •

I bought my first (and only) ATVs for my wife and myself in 1986, and we have used them constantly ever since. I have found that if you drive them sensibly, they are a very definite asset. When I am hunting deer, elk, or antelope, 90 percent of the time I am in first or second gear, just above an idle, and have driven within forty yards of all species. I see a lot more country as well as more game. When you go hell-bent for leather, slide around, and tear up the countryside, you don't see nearly as much of anything. Also, that is where ATVs get their bad name. Slow the darned things down, and smell the daisies.

Tony Hafen
St. George, Utah

• • •

Elk definitely begin to head closer to the trees when they hear those motors coming up the trail, even if it is still dark and you're two miles away. Be considerate of your fellow hunters who may have already hiked up in the dark or camped near those good feeding areas. If you had put in the effort to hike in or camp out, you wouldn't want some lazy hunter scaring the elk into the trees before it's even light enough to shoot.

I highly recommend leaving the ATV in camp during early morning—including the pre-dawn—until several hours after shooting light. If you must use an ATV to get closer to that honey-hole, ride in during the middle of the day and set up a cold camp within a mile or so. You will significantly increase your odds of success and decrease the chance of ruining someone else's hunt.

Troy Wiescamp
Longmont, Colorado

• • •

Yes, elk associate ATVs with danger. And just listen how far away you can hear an ATV; an elk can hear a lot farther. We've bowhunted public lands in Colorado that had a lot of ATVs traveling on and off roads. When the ATVs were thick, it was hard to find elk even in the deepest, darkest canyons. One year when there was only one other camp besides ours in the area, and no ATVs, we saw elk every day and killed two. Because the ATVs have gotten worse, we have moved to an area that is walk-in only. There isn't a single ATV in the area, and elk everywhere. Yes, ATVs are a liability. Get yourself in shape and leave your ATVs at home. It makes better hunting for everyone.

Verlyn Mahan
Greeley, Colorado

I believe elk sense even distant ATV sounds as a threat and react as they would to any danger, by putting more distance between them and the ATV. I once watched a good royal bull feeding steadily toward me for ten minutes. He was still out of range when an ATV passed down a trail far behind me. We both heard it. I remained still, but the bull deliberately moved off at a right angle. It was a beautiful animal. Smart, too.

John Vieira
Palisade, Colorado

• • •

I hunted elk in Oregon for more than thirty years and my information is from personal observation, not science. I have a stand along an elk corridor that feeds across a small meadow. I have watched hunters on ATVs cross the meadow, stop and glass the area, then ride away. On several occasions, within minutes of their departure, elk have appeared in the meadow en route to cover in front of my stand. I don't know what kind of success the guys on ATVs are having, but I have consistently put elk in my freezer.

Brian Burgess
Medford, Oregon

In my experience, elk won't tolerate an ATV, and the most successful hunters are those who walk. But don't tell the ATV crowd. Let them keep complaining about not seeing any game.

Max Keisel
Richfield, Utah

• • •

On an elk-hunting trip in Colorado several years ago, my friends and I had lunch at a spot overlooking a canyon. We spotted a group of elk bedded down in some aspens, just fifty yards from a road running down the bottom of the canyon. We could see about half a mile of road, and a pickup was just coming into view. We were amazed as it went right past the elk. Apparently nobody in the pickup saw the elk, and the elk remained bedded. Fifteen minutes later a Jeep came down the road and went back up with the same results. A few minutes later yet another truck came and went, and the elk just stayed put. We were all talking about how the other hunters could not see the elk lying in plain sight, when all of a sudden the elk jumped up and ran out of the canyon as if they had been poked with a cattle prod. Soon an ATV came into view, driving down the road. The elk disappeared over the ridge before the ATV rider had a chance to see them.

Apparently just the sound of the ATV drove the elk out of the canyon. We surmised that this explained why the game pole at the camp with all the ATVs had been empty most years.

My advice to ATV owners is to leave them at camp and only use them for recovering game after the kill, and even then, not drive them off designated roads and trails.

Jim Brunner
Lincoln, Nebraska

When an elk is killed in warm weather in remote country with only walk-in access, and it will take a couple of days to pack it out, what is the best way to preserve the meat? How can you tell if the meat is spoiled?

Scott Frost
Embudo, New Mexico

• • •

Our group of five cooperates on the pack-outs to get all the meat out in one trip. Once in camp, we reduce the meat to smaller cuts and put it on ice in large ice chests.

You will know when meat has spoiled—
you can smell it.

Leland Geistweidt
Fredericksburg, Texas

• • •

Get the prize out of direct sunlight and out of
direct contact with the ground. Trim away
wound-edges and bloodshot meat. If body fluids
or digestive tract contents get on meat, rinse
thoroughly or trim away the affected area. Apply
black pepper liberally. Don't use plastic or artificial fabric for meat bags except for a very short
time. Don't sack up the meat at all until it has
cooled. Insulate cooled meat with a sleeping bag
or blankets in the daytime. Suspend meat over a
cool flowing stream if available, or place bagged
meat directly in the stream. If necessary, you can
cool sacked meat in the earth for a time. Seal
game bags from the dirt with leaves, grass, or layers of cotton.

John Vieira
Palisade, Colorado

• • •

First, check the regulations. Some states require
that the reproductive organs or udder remain

naturally attached to a quarter during transport.

If my hunt is successful, I will need eight cheesecloth game bags; a good sharp knife, folding saw and hatchet; fifty to seventy-five feet of parachute cord; and cayenne and black pepper mixed in equal measure—the more the better.

Removing the hide is the first step toward releasing the animal's body heat. Spread the hide on each side for a clean working surface. Separate the shoulders and hind quarters from the carcass. Remove the backstrap, tenderloin, ribs, and neck, rubbing each with pepper mix to keep the flies and wasps at bay. Hang the sacked meat in the shade, and separate sacks so air can circulate.

John Garrick
Crescent, Oregon

• • •

Field-dress, skin, and quarter the animal immediately to get the heat out of the carcass. Hang the meat in the shade, even if it means carrying it some distance. Air movement over meat acts like an evaporative cooler. After several training sessions on game meat inspection, I've learned that if it looks good and smells good, it is good.

John V. Toman
North Bend, Oregon

Skin it as soon as you can. Quarter it, and if possible hang the quarters in a tree that will be in the shade all day. Put pepper all over it, and the flies will not bother it. You will be able to tell if it is spoiled by the smell.

Larry Breitbach
Port Angeles, Washington

• • •

Quarter it, skin it, and hang it in a tree or on a meat pole. Cover it with game bags and put pepper on it to keep the flies away. Keep it in the shade.

Don't let the hind quarters lie together for long. I have seen spoiled hind quarters in Montana in late January. The temperature that night was very warm for that time of year—about thirty-five above zero. The bull was left lying on the ground overnight with the hind quarters on top of each other. The meat smelled bad the next day and was also somewhat slimy.

David W. Stewart
East Helena, Montana

Skin and quarter your kill at once. Put up a meat pole in the shade if possible, and hang the quarters so they won't touch each other. They should lose all the body heat overnight. Cover loosely with a tarp or manti at night, and tie the cover tightly around the meat during the day to keep it from warming up. If it's raining, keep it as dry as possible. It also helps to trim all loose flaps and any meat that's bloodshot. Pepper and/or cheesecloth will keep the flies to a minimum.

If you're backpacking, by all means bone out the meat. A bull elk will average a hundred lbs. per dressed quarter, and a cow seventy-five lbs. The less inedible weight you have to pack for any distance, the better.

As to spoiled meat, it gets slick and shiny, and the smell, even early on, should leave you no doubt.

Jim Jennings
Kaslo, British Columbia

I often face one- to two-hour climbs before daylight in freezing weather to reach prime elk hunting locations. I'd like to know how other hunters avoid, or manage, overheating during a strenuous climb. I'm reluctant to climb slower and add additional time to the trip, but if I get up any earlier I'll hardly have time for sleep. Any suggestions?

Bruce E. Hostrander
Painted Post, New York

The solution lies in a larger-than-usual daypack stuffed with an entire set of dry clothes. Hike uphill lightly dressed, for heat comes easily with exertion. Cotton is fine; it'll be coming off. Upon reaching your destination, strip to the skin. Remove your shorts, socks, everything that's become damp from perspiration. It's still dark, so nothing to be embarrassed about. Let the cold north wind dry your skin until a light chill sets in. Then put on your fresh next-to-skin layer of clothing. In a few minutes, or as soon as you feel chilly enough to need it, add an insulating layer, then—slowly now, if needed—a heavier vest or jacket. Then put on a hat, gloves or mittens, and boots. Wet clothing goes into the pack. To keep any of its scent from escaping, put the wet clothes in a plastic bag and seal it before stuffing it into your pack. You're now set for a warm and wonderful day of hunting.

Allan Reishus, M.D.
Craig, Colorado

• • •

The key to avoiding overheating during long climbs in freezing weather is to dress in layers. I like to start my climbs just a bit cold. As my body produces heat, I can shed layers to prevent sweating. I put those extra layers in my pack. When I reach my destination, or as temperatures decrease, I put those extra layers back on. With today's high-tech, lightweight materials, you can keep comfortable without having to carry too much weight and bulk. Avoid cotton because once it's wet, it stays wet and will chill you instead of warming you.

Rick Moberly
Mammoth Lakes, California

• • •

Check out the new lines of clothing, especially the undergarments that wick away body sweat. Dress in layers and start with no heavy coat on. Wait until you are at your destination to put on extra garments. Warm, dry footwear is just as important. I use Schnee's Hunter boots, and I prefer wool for pants, coat, and cap.

Body heat goes out the top of your head. Use a light cap or no cap when hiking, then put on a warm one when you slow down or stop. In states that require it, remember to keep plenty of hunter orange showing when it's daylight.

Dennis Tandberg
Harlowton, Montana

It's very important to dress in layers. At the first sign of overheating, I start to dress down. Merino wool underwear tops and bottoms have worked well for me. They keep me warm even when damp and dry out fast when I stop sweating.

It also helps to get in shape before hunting season by running stairs or walking uphill grades. I don't sweat as easily or as much if I'm in shape.

Randy Hanish
Park Falls, Wisconsin

• • •

The way I handle the long walk from camp to my hunting area is to pack my long underwear and sweater in my backpack. Then I tie my jacket around my waist. It is a little cool when I first start out, but the work of hiking will keep me warm. Then when I get to my spot for the day, I re-dress with all my long underwear and sweater. I have adapted much of my hunting clothing to things I learned many years ago in survival school, such as wearing wool which keeps you warm even when wet.

M.Sgt. Ray Wiebe
Peterson AFB, Colorado

I learned a trick when I was at the Navy's Survival Evasion and Resistance (SERE) school in Brunswick, Maine. If you are going to hike a long distance in cold weather, dress down until you are "comfortably" cool. Usually it means taking off your jacket and/or heavy-weather clothing and lashing it to your pack, but keeping your head and hands well-covered. The first feeling you may get is that you are too cold. However, once you start moving and your body starts to warm up, you will reach a good balance of staying warm without overheating, and without the nuisance of excessive sweat. Once you get to your desired location and begin to feel chilly, you can easily don your parka and continue on with your hunt.

Lt. Matt Williams, U.S. Navy

• • •

If there's no time constraint, why not pack the bare essentials you'll need to overnight, and leave late on the afternoon before? You'll have a daylight climb, and then just wake up among them. Shoot your elk, then climb out of your sleeping bag.

Jim Nichols
Billings, Montana

What is the most effective way to hunt bull elk after the rut is done and gone, and once it gets really cold?

Harper Summers
Albuquerque, New Mexico

• • •

After the rut has passed, the mature herd bull will leave the cows seeking a place that's secure and quiet to regain some of his strength and fill his stomach. Look for that place of solitude that hunters won't likely venture into, a place with water and thick timber pockets close to grassy south slopes several miles from roads.

If you find the hideout and there are several smaller bulls in a group, you may be tempted to take one. To shoot the big mature bull, the one in your dreams, you will need to search deeper into the hideout, as he will often stay away from other elk.

Rusty South
Great Falls, Montana

• • •

Most bulls that were active during the rut will go off by themselves or in small, all-bull groups to eat and rest. You have to do a lot of glassing to locate lone bulls in the open parks, as well as in the thick timber. Sometimes a "dark hole" bull will stay in the thick stuff and eat evergreen needles. They like to stay off by themselves, but I have had them come in silently and even answer to cow talk and bugles after the rut. Extremely cold weather will cause an elk to do unexpected things and show up in odd places, so be alert.

Dennis Tandberg
Harlowton, Montana

• • •

Where we hunt, if it's cold there's snow. We look for fresh bull tracks, and once we find some we stay on them till we find the elk. Sometimes you win and sometimes you lose.

Frank James
Bozeman, Montana

• • •

Sometimes old bulls don't leave their post-rut hideouts until long after the last gunshot of the season. But if you find a large group of cows, yearlings, spikes, and raghorns, there's a fair chance some mature bulls are hanging out within a mile or two of them. Go farther back and higher up, and look for big tracks. If you find a group of tracks with no calf tracks, it's almost certainly a bunch of bulls. If you find tracks of one elk traveling alone, it's probably a bull. Sometimes it's hard to tell a moose track from a bull elk track in deep snow. Know the difference between their tracks, droppings, and urine scent.

Cougar Jones
Reno, Nevada

• • •

A bedded bull is very difficult to sneak up on any time of the year, but a feeding elk is relatively easy to approach as long as he can't wind you.

Cold weather and approaching winter storms will drive elk to feed with less caution than usual. Most hunters get really excited when the weatherman announces the approach of a storm. They plan their hunts for immediately after the storm because they know there will be good tracking snow. However, I much prefer the afternoon and evening before the storm. Bull elk sense the coming of the storm and know they have to stoke up on groceries to last it out. It is very common to find elk feeding in open areas in early afternoon just before a storm arrives, and these elk are often not wary or observant because they are so intent on feeding.

John Flynn
Townsend, Montana

• • •

Big, old, still-healthy bull elk are, generally speaking, lazy almost all of the time, and more so after the rut. When the rut is over they are usually holed up alone and doing almost nothing but eating and sleeping. They hang out close to water, and feed in places where there's the least chance of being disturbed—not necessarily in thick timber, or miles from roads, but in places where they've hardly ever seen or felt threatened by a human being. Really cold weather keeps them up feeding longer, and may coax them to spend a little more time out on sunny, open ground. If you can find a place that's likely to appeal to such an animal, and there's an open (usually south-facing) slope nearby, with some grass in it, and you find some big, fresh tracks or droppings in it or around its edges, that'd be a good place to set up an ambush before daylight, or just before dark.

Steve Hopkins
Tucson, Arizona

• • •

During our November rifle seasons, it will often snap very cold after a big snowstorm. I remember catching horses for the day's hunt when it was nine degrees below zero with two feet of snow on the ground. We saw 140 elk that day, but no mature bulls. Sometimes it's tempting to think that all the big ones have been shot out, because you'll see a herd of sixty head with only a few spikes representing the males of the species. Not true. They just choose to hang out elsewhere. In our particular neck of the woods, that means above the girls and the little boys. You may think two feet of snow will push the elk down, but it won't. The big bulls stay up there either solo or in small bachelor bunches, and they won't come down until winter is very severe. If you want one of the big bulls, you'll have to ride or hike higher into the mountains, through deep snow, until you find tracks or spot one feeding early in the morning. They're there; they're just higher up, harder to find, tougher, and worth it.

Gary Hubbell
Marble, Colorado

I live at about 100 feet above sea level and hunt elk in Colorado. Waking up at almost sea level and going to bed that night at 10,000 feet gives me a headache and nausea. I'd much rather spend mornings looking for a big bull than tossing my cookies outside the tent. My schedule doesn't allow me to acclimate slowly. I drink plenty of water but am allergic to Diamox. Anyone know of a remedy for my altitude sickness?

Bob Recupero
Ferrisburgh, Vermont

Altitude sickness is caused by the heavy breathing needed to get necessary oxygen out of "thinner" air. A secondary effect of this heavy breathing is blowing off carbon dioxide from the lungs and blood which changes the pH of the blood. This causes the headache and nausea. The solution is to take three to six antacids like Tums or Rolaids a day for two or three days before your trip and the first couple of days in the mountains. These help keep blood pH at normal levels despite the carbon dioxide being blown off.

The spleen pumps extra red blood cells into the blood within twenty-four hours of hitting the mountains, and the red blood cells help you get the oxygen you need without hyperventilating. That is part of the reason you are normally feeling a little better after two or three days at altitude. The antacid solution works for me—we camp at 9,000 feet and go up from there.

Timothy J. Boyle
Dakota Dunes, South Dakota

• • •

I worked for an oxygen company in Wyoming for years, and every fall we handed out a lot of oxygen bottles for people with the same problem.

Go to your doctor and have him write a prescription for oxygen as needed, at one to two liters per minute. Wear it to bed the first one or two nights while getting used to the altitude, and if feeling sick. Any oxygen company should be able to rent you a couple of tanks for around fifty to a hundred dollars up front. Some insurance companies will cover it.

A physical exam before going is a good idea also. If you feel so sick you puke before you hike or pack an elk, you may have more than altitude problems.

Sean Orszulak
Casper, Wyoming

• • •

I read an article in a Colorado conservation magazine about twenty years ago, written by a doctor, who said that there was an ingredient in the original Rolaids tablets that lessened, and even suppressed, the effects of altitude sickness. I live at sea level year-round, and have hunted at elevations of 8,000 to 9,000 feet in northern New Mexico for the past eighteen years. I chew a couple Rolaids when I start out on the hunt, and when I am walking hard or exerting myself heavily I pop another one or two into my mouth and chew them. I have never had any problem with altitude sickness.

C. J. Baker
Paulina, Louisiana

• • •

Living in New York and hunting in Colorado for a dozen years, I found it helpful to train aerobically as aggressively as I could (running uphill, for example) at home before the hunt. You might also look for a health club that has sealed chambers around their running machines; oxygen levels inside the chambers can be adjusted to match high-altitude conditions.

John A. Cleveland
Denver, Colorado

• • •

Being a flatlander from Indiana, I have experienced the same thing. I began increasing my exercise regimen to help my recovery rate, so my body wouldn't think it was working so hard. This has helped me with more than just altitude sickness.

I also take a multi-vitamin with iron. I read that iron helps the red blood cells maximize their oxygen-carrying capacity. (I learned not to be excessive with the iron; that can cause other problems.) Finally, the first day of the hunt I search areas that are less demanding and work into the more strenuous areas.

This combination has helped me immensely. I still get minor headaches, but no nausea. The headaches are easily manageable with acetaminophen. I am not a doctor, just another hunter trying to figure it out. Good luck.

Rob Koon
Granger, Indiana

• • •

Eat a high-carbohydrate diet with more than 70 percent of your calories coming from starches (bread, potatoes, pasta, rice, etc.). Drink plenty of fluids—enough so that your urine is a very light yellow to almost clear. Do not drink alcohol; it dehydrates the body and decreases the breathing drive when sleeping, thus worsening altitude sickness. Do not take sleeping pills, which also decrease the breathing drive while sleeping.

The best drug alternative to Diamox (acetazolamide) is Decadron (a steroid). A prescription is needed, and like all medications it has its side effects, which include increased irritability, insomnia, and elevated blood sugar. The recommended dose is one four-mg tablet every six hours, starting twelve hours before your trip and continuing while at altitude or for approximately three to five days until you have acclimated to the altitude. Other positive effects of Decadron are that it can increase your energy, ease aching joints, and relieve poison ivy symptoms.

Some studies have shown that Ginkgo biloba helps prevent altitude sickness, while other studies have not shown a benefit. A suggested dose is sixty mg, three times daily, starting five days before ascending and continuing while at altitude. If nausea, vomiting, and headache persist despite any of the above treatments, descend rapidly before high-altitude cerebral edema (swelling of the brain) develops.

Don Gibbon
Indiana, Pennsylvania

• • •

I've hunted elk in Colorado for forty-five years and for the last thirty-five years have backpacked four miles in and 800 feet up to our campsite—and packed meat and antlers out. Everyone we've had in our camp gets tired, but one hunter became nauseated and continued to feel bad for two or three days. He attributed his condition to age, being out of shape, etc. I had always carried antacid tablets for indigestion, and that being the only "medicine" in camp that seemed like it might possibly help him, I offered him some. He chewed three or four, and within hours felt great and continued to feel okay the rest of the week.

The following year he was again feeling nauseated. Again he took some Rolaids and felt okay. From then on, we made sure we had them with us. Later, I read an article about high-altitude sickness and learned that a person's blood becomes more acidic at higher altitudes. The article suggested that antacids would help adjust the blood pH and specifically mentioned Rolaids. Apparently we had accidentally stumbled on their remedy. Rolaids may not be the answer for everyone, but we definitely are convinced that it makes a big difference.

Dwayne Lyles
Centennial, Colorado

• • •

I, too, live just a few miles from the ocean and hunt Colorado with very little time to acclimate. I used to get violently ill after the first day of hard hunting—a horrible headache with bouts of vomiting. I've found that while Diamox does the trick, it has a very serious impact on my vision, starting a couple of days after I begin taking it and lasting several days after I stop.

Even with my tight schedule, I make sure I get to altitude with enough time to go for a modest hike the evening before hunting. This at least starts the acclimation process. I take ibuprofen for the headache and Tums for the nausea before starting out each morning, and again midday and at night. These do a pretty good job of preventing the altitude sickness symptoms from starting up. Finally, I save the toughest areas to hunt for day three or beyond, taking it just a little easy on the first day or two of hunting.

Jon Strebler
Chula Vista, California

• • •

Being a "flatlander" from Louisiana, I also suffered from altitude sickness that kept me out of action for a couple of days whenever we went to our cabin at 9,000 feet near Black Canyon in Colorado. Then a friend from Colorado gave me this suggestion: starting about twenty-four hours before I will be at high altitude, I take a full dose of regular aspirin. The thinking is that low oxygen causes the altitude-related symptoms, and aspirin thins your blood and allows better oxygen delivery. I don't know if that's true, but it has worked for me going on five years now. I don't take aspirin all day, just a couple of regular-strength tablets on the way to Colorado, and then two a day on the first couple of days up there. It has made the difference between lying around and getting out to scout for the elk.

Susie Fair
Mansfield, Louisiana

• • •

My wife and I live in Florida and have a home in Leadville, Colorado (elevation 10,200 feet). For a long time, each time we went we experienced different symptoms and tried different things. One time we used Ginkgo biloba (250 mg, four times a day) starting four weeks before the trip. This helped me, but my wife still had symptoms. We both now take over-the-counter diuretics and drink plenty of water. No headaches and no nausea. I should also state we do not drink any alcohol prior to the trip, and once there we wait one day before having any. Hope this helps.

Andrew Kaldany
Bonita Springs, Florida

As a former mountain climber I learned a few tricks. First, a few months (and especially the last few weeks) before your trip, condition your body to altitude changes by spending a couple of nights at the highest elevation point you can drive to each weekend.

Second, for the month prior to your trip—longer if you can—spend thirty to forty minutes, three days a week, doing something to keep your heart rate in your target zone. You can find your target zone by subtracting your age from 220. This will give you a number. Now multiply this number by .80 and by .60. The result you get by the .80 will be your maximum heart rate of your target zone. The .60 result will be your minimum heart rate of your target zone. By keeping your heart rate within this zone during the month-long regimen, you build up your heart muscles to meet the demand of high altitude.

Last, take one aspirin at eight-hour intervals, starting one day before your departure until three days after you arrive. These tips worked for me even when I could not work out on a continual basis. As the Boy Scouts say, "Be Prepared."

Bruce Nyberg
Sheridan, Wyoming

Altitude sickness, more properly known as acute mountain sickness (AMS), is a pretty miserable condition to endure. It's like one's worst-ever hangover without the memories of some wild times the night before.

First, I would ask if somehow a schedule could be arranged to allow for at least some acclimation. Full acclimation will take about three weeks, but much benefit comes from just two or three days. Perhaps a day and night in Denver at 5,200 feet, followed by a day or two in one of Colorado's delightful mountain towns at 7,500 feet, could be arranged. That would lessen the AMS symptoms (but not eliminate them).

Next, I question if there is a true allergy to Diamox (acetazolamide). Tingling sensations in the hands and feet and taste-bud alterations are common side effects and not allergic symptoms. The side effects can be tolerated, and usually get better even if Diamox is continued. True allergy to Diamox, or any sulfa antibiotic drug, to which Diamox is closely related, means that Diamox must be avoided. True allergy symptoms include a hives-like skin rash or wheezing. If Diamox cannot be taken, another drug option is Decadron (dexamethasone) taken in four-mg tablets three or four times daily. Either medicine should be begun a full day prior to reaching altitude and continued for four or five days.

General measures to minimize AMS include the "hike high, sleep low" motto of mountain climbers. If possible, hike or drive downhill to camp. Even a 500- or 1,000-foot lower sleeping altitude will make a difference. Drinking plenty of water, avoiding salty foods, and avoiding alcohol are also useful measures.

Allan Reishus, M.D.
Craig, Colorado

• • •

I've read articles about Viagra being used to combat edema and altitude sickness in climbers in the Himalayas. This could be the answer for you. You might want to give your hunting partners a heads-up, though.

Tony Hoyt
Arlee, Montana

• • •

Don't consume any caffeine for at least a month before you hunt at high altitude. This means staying away from coffee, tea, cocoa, and soda pop. Also eliminate any food or beverage that contains aspartame. And abstain from using tobacco and alcohol. Finally, you might try the wristbands that are used to help with car and airplane (motion) sickness.

Dennis Tandberg
Harlowton, Montana

• • •

Two weeks before you go, start taking one ibuprofen dose a day. The ibuprofen thins your blood. After moving into a home at 9,000 feet, it took us several months to acclimate.

Earl Fox
Westcliffe, Colorado

• • •

There is an extremely easy answer to altitude sickness: stop hunting at 10,000 feet. There are plenty of elk and other game to hunt at 5,000 feet. Key to hunting ethics, safety, and comfort is realizing your limits and not exceeding them. You may need to change hunting partners, hire a guide, or make other sacrifices to change your hunting area. You will be better off.

Bob Hoffmann
Moscow, Idaho

Two to three weeks before you leave to hunt, start taking two aspirin a day, and then drink as much water as you can. Continue this for at least two days after you arrive. I have never had any problem with altitude sickness since I started this.

Lane Jacobson
Rockville, Minnesota

• • •

Take 120 mg Ginkgo biloba daily, starting five days before departure and continue for the duration of your trip. It has worked for me on three occasions. It may also help mental sharpness, which I can always use.

Doug Davis
Glen Ellen, California

• • •

There is probably nothing you can do to avoid a headache and nausea that first night. But you might be able to reduce the severity by avoiding caffeine, alcohol, greasy foods, and exertion until you are acclimated. These things all affect the amount of oxygenated blood that reaches your brain. A brain low on oxygen is what makes you sick. Your body compensates by increasing your respiration rate, and by changing the pH of your blood so that it can absorb additional oxygen, which takes time.

You can also speed your acclimatization by getting in better aerobic shape. The more efficiently your body processes oxygen at sea level, the less you will suffer at altitude. If you have some spare change, you can purchase one of the systems that professional athletes use to simulate training at altitude. Some are portable devices you strap to your face, while some are as big as a wall tent that you sleep inside. Do an Internet search on "altitude training" to learn more. And keep pounding the water!

Kurt Cox
Golden, Colorado

When an elk is shot, does it have a tendency to run uphill, downhill, or sidehill? I have heard many different stories and think this would be helpful for finding an animal under poor tracking conditions and with only a small amount of blood to follow.

Dave Graber
Marietta, Ohio

• • •

When shot, an elk is liable to run in any direction, depending on where it was hit. The only way to find it is to track it, and you will be amazed!

Wounded elk are just as unpredictable as ever. About the time you think you have them figured out, you find you are wrong. You might think an injured elk would take the path of least resistance. You will revise that thought when you track an elk into a thicket so dense you have to crawl through, only to be led into Blowdown City.

When the tracks turn downhill, your sigh of relief may be short-lived, for you may soon find where the elk turned back up the hill and went over the ridge into another drainage. Huffing and puffing at the ridgetop, your "Why Didn't Is" start." "Why didn't I take more time placing my shot?" "Why didn't I just stop and get steady before pulling the trigger?" "Why me, Lord?"

John Garrick
Crescent City, Oregon

• • •

The direction an elk runs after being shot has a lot to do with where it was hit, how much knock-down power was left in the bullet at impact, and also the terrain. With shoulder hits, an elk will usually dip in the front end on impact and go downhill. A lung shot sometimes looks like a miss because the bullet doesn't knock them over but passes right through and doesn't spend all its energy on the elk. A lung-shot elk can run any direction. If there are other elk, they sometimes go with the herd until they slow down for lack of oxygen. Then they usually just lie down or stand with spraddled legs until they lose consciousness and fall. Paunch and liver hits will make them hunch up. Again they can go any direction and are able to travel much farther than if shot through the lungs. Heart shots will sometimes make them jump or rear up on their hind legs. They won't go far before lying down. Remember, though, there is always the exception to the rule. Keep your eye on the animal you shot at. Be ready to shoot again if needed.

Dennis Tandberg
Harlowton, Montana

• • •

I have taken quite a few elk and have helped track elk hit by rifles large and small. A shot from a .270 or larger round with a premium bullet can break the front shoulder and penetrate to the vitals. Every elk shot in that manner goes down on the spot or goes downhill. Other than this, all bets are off.

A premium bullet will increase the odds of a pass-through shot and a better chance of a good blood trail. If hit too far back, the soft tissue of the abdomen can close the wound and stop the free flow of blood. I once tracked a bull about 400 yards sidehill and uphill after it was shot through the liver. We knew the hit was too far back and so waited until the next day to track. We had very little blood at first and even less after fifty yards. I found that bull by good old-fashioned tracking and thinking about escape cover. Most experienced elk hunters will tell you that elk always seem to die in the worst possible spot for field dressing and retrieval.

If you have very little blood to follow, back off and wait a few hours. If you push the animal too soon, it may go for miles. Most important of all, look at the land and think: What's the best escape route? Where's the thickest cover?

Jerry Lisenbee
Cheyenne, Wyoming

• • •

Our hunting party has killed more than eighty bull elk in the last twenty-four years. Of course, some of these elk did not hit the ground for keeps after they were shot. My experience is that elk will try to escape danger in any direction they think is most directly away from where you are. Break their leg and they will run uphill as likely as down. Running to cover is a likely move; elk in our area favor a jack-fir patch or alder draw.

Developing an "all day" tracking attitude is a must. Don't give up when the blood trail slows to a drop every few yards. Carry flagging ribbon and mark where you saw the last blood spot. Start circling until you find more blood. (Pick up the flagging when you're done.) Whatever you do, don't make noise or talk loudly. The elk will hear you coming, get up, and move out. Keep going even when you want to give up, and most likely you will be rewarded with an elk in the freezer.

Doug Coplen
Hoodsport, Washington

• • •

I have seen elk run both downhill and uphill after being shot and shot at. In my experience they seem to generally run directly away from the threat. It also seems to me that they quite often run for heavy, dense cover. Their hooves definitely disturb the ground, leaving a trail that's not too hard to see with or without blood—at least until they stop running.

Mike Nault
Thornton, Colorado

• • •

I have found that elk do one of two things when hit. First, they mostly run downhill. Second, they tend to run back in the direction that they came from—back to where everything was okay.

In tracking the animal, consider the speed at which the elk takes off running. An elk that takes off at full speed when it is hit can go a hundred yards or more in a very short time. Several years ago we tracked an elk down one hill, up another hill, and down the backside before finding it. We were amazed to see that it was shot right through the heart and lungs.

You may want to purchase one of those lights, such as the one made by Gerber, that helps you see small amounts of blood.

Jim Hawkins
Coeur d'Alene, Idaho

Elk hit well in the vitals will almost always go downhill. They may "spook" uphill for a short distance, but my experience has been they soon turn and go downhill. With a well-placed shot, the recovery distance is normally less than fifty yards, whatever hunting method you're using.

Pinkish, foamy blood is a sure sign of a lung shot and meat in the freezer. However, even blood that is not aerated can mean a successful shot and must be followed up. A dedicated elk hunter will track wounded game for days if need be to ensure he/she has not left a dead elk in the woods. If an elk is not hit well, you could be in for a long day or two, as the elk may take you up, down, and across the terrain. The secret is to only shoot when you are sure you can make a clean, quick kill.

John Frerich
Newcastle, Washington

• • •

In my experience, the answer to the question is "yes." I have seen wounded elk move in all directions. In each case there was an explanation for the direction and distance the elk traveled. Factors that influence the elk's route include the type and extent of the wound, the direction the other elk in the herd went, the terrain and cover, and the best direction for the elk to feel safe and away from the source of danger (if known to the elk). I have seen an elk go in a combination of directions and even in the equivalent of a circle. I have seen an elk just lay back down in cover a few feet away. Watch. Be still. Don't be in a hurry. Think. Analyze what is going on. Get help.

John T. Mercer
McMinnville, Oregon

• • •

Understanding what direction an elk (and most other animals) will travel after being shot begins with understanding how natural funnels—features of the land that catch and direct movement into a narrowing flow—influence animals' daily movements. Natural funnels may be canyons, ravines, gulches, swales, margins of rivers and lakes, or saddles between mountain peaks—all routes of least resistance. Remember that conservation of energy often determines if a living organism will survive. Animals, including elk, use these easier routes whenever they can.

When an animal is shot, it will instinctively use these same routes, but its behavior will be influenced by what means the injury was inflicted. Firearms, for instance, kill by producing severe shock and tissue/organ damage. An animal shot in a vital area of the body with a weapon of this type will react to the fear, trauma, and almost instantaneous body weakening by traveling the route of least resistance as quickly as it can. If there is slope to the terrain, the animal will commonly go downhill.

On the other hand, an elk shot with an arrow may at first feel nothing except for a sudden poke or punch. The internal organs do not have nerve endings. The cutting edges of the broadhead are (or should be) razor sharp, so pain where the arrow enters and exits is not instantly experienced. Because death occurs by internal hemorrhaging, with virtually no trauma, an elk may simply continue in the direction— uphill, sidehill, or downhill—that it was originally traveling. However, as it weakens from blood loss, this behavior will change and the animal will then begin following the route of least resistance.

A broken front leg may cause an animal to travel uphill; the powerful hind legs and weight distribution to the rear portion of the body make it easier for the wounded animal to move in this direction. After distancing itself from the immediate danger, it may then begin traveling downhill. Even though this changes the weight distribution to the front, where the injury is, it's still using less energy to go downhill.

An animal with a broken hind leg will generally travel downhill, as the efficiency of those powerful hind legs has been compromised and the weight distribution to the front part of the body makes downhill travel easier. An animal that has been shot in the liver or guts will, if left alone, soon find a hiding spot in heavy cover and lie down.

The route is also influenced by whether or not the antagonist has been seen. An animal that has seen the hunter will react differently from one that hasn't; namely, it will more likely choose a route that best helps it distance and shield itself from the hunter. This factor is more important if the animal is wounded in a nonlethal or not instantly lethal part of the body, and thus has more awareness, energy, and options.

Track every animal shot, even if it falls within sight. By doing so, you're teaching yourself to read animal sign, and the more you can learn, the easier it will be for you to find the animal that will some day give you the ultimate challenge.

Richard Hayes

Chattaroy, Washington

INDEX

ABOUT THE ROCKY MOUNTAIN ELK FOUNDATION

Founded in 1984 and headquartered in Missoula, Montana, the Rocky Mountain Elk Foundation is a nonprofit organization dedicated to ensuring the future of elk, other wildlife and their habitat. The Elk Foundation and its partners have permanently protected or enhanced more than 4.5 million acres, a land area nearly twice as large as Yellowstone National Park—and opened to public access more than 450,000 acres previously closed to hunting, fishing, and other recreation. The Elk Foundation upholds the hunting tradition by protecting places where wild animals will continue to thrive and people will continue to hunt. We strongly support and encourage hunting practiced with respect for the individual animal, the species, and the land. We believe that honest hunting for free-ranging animals kindles vitality in the individual hunter, deepens appreciation of wildlife and wildlands, and strengthens society as a whole.

To help protect wild elk country or learn more about the Rocky Mountain Elk Foundation, visit www.elkfoundation.org or call 800-CALL-ELK.

ABOUT THE EDITOR

Don Burgess's stories and articles have appeared frequently in *Bugle* magazine since 1987, and he has been *Bugle's* hunting editor since 1997. A passionate elk hunter and proud life member of the Rocky Mountain Elk Foundation, Don has been immersed in elk hunting and elk lore since his dad first introduced him to a bugling bull in the Bitterroot Mountains of western Montana in 1952. He and his wife, Jan, live in Florence, Montana.

Our *Bugle* hats are off to Dennis Tandberg and John Vieira for sharing so much of their knowledge with *Bugle* readers and allowing us to include it in this book.